OSC IB STUDY & REVISION GUIDES
FOR THE INTERNATIONAL BACCALAUREATE DIPLOMA PROGRAMME

History

Paper 2: Authoritarian States
Russia 1917–1953

Standard and Higher Level

Joe Gauci

FSC

OSC IB Study and Revision Guides
Published by OSC Publishing,
Belsyre Court, 57 Woodstock Road,
Oxford OX2 6HJ, UK

History
Paper 2: Authoritarian States Russia 1917–1953
Standard and Higher Level
© 2017 Joe Gauci
9781910689363
363.02

The material in this Study and Revision Guide has been developed independently of the International Baccalaureate Organisation. OSC IB Study and Revision Guides are available in most major IB subject areas. Full details of all our current titles, prices and sample pages as well as future releases are available on our website.

Cover and Chapter Openings Image: Isaak Brodsky [Public domain], via Wikimedia Commons

How to order

Orders can be made via the website, e-mail, fax, phone or mail;
contact numbers and addresses below.

OSC
Belsyre Court, 57 Woodstock Road
Oxford OX2 6HJ, UK
T : +44 (0) 1865 512802
F : +44 (0) 1865 512335
E : osc@osc-ib.com
W: osc-ib.com

Printed and bound by CPI Group (UK) Ltd, Croydon CR0 4YY
www.cpibooks.co.uk

MIX
Paper from
responsible sources
FSC
www.fsc.org **FSC® C013604**

Preface

I have taught History for the past thirty years in independent schools in the UK, including teaching the IB for twenty-three years at Malvern College, as well as teaching on OSC Spring Revision and Summer Schools for the past twenty years. I am never happier than when discussing approaches to key historical questions with students and exchanging ideas about different perspectives that can be taken on the past. So, working on this study guide has been a real pleasure and I have tried to take approaches in writing it that my experience over the past thirty years has shown work best in preparing students to tackle essay questions.

I have always enjoyed writing history essays and helping students prepare for essay-based examination papers. For history students, generally essay-writing is the biggest challenge they will face. Writing a very good or excellent essay requires both a very secure understanding of a lot of historical information and a mastery of a range of essay-writing skills such as: interpreting the question; planning an effective approach to the question and creating a clear structure; writing an introduction that identifies the themes or factors the essay will explore and the thesis of the essay; developing a clear line of argument and keeping focused on the title; selecting and deploying precisely an appropriate range of supporting evidence; restating the main argument of the essay in order to provide a strong conclusion.

How to Use This Guide

In terms of technique, the guide starts with a section of advice on how to approach essay questions. In addition, I have provided practice essay questions, partially completed by me but with space for you to have a go at too.

This guide contains detailed notes on the emergence and rule of Lenin and Stalin's authoritarian state in Russia. There are 'Key Term' boxes throughout the guide, providing information relating to key terms and definitions which are important to know when studying Soviet Russia. There are also 'Key Historical Perspectives' sections which explain important debates among historians about Soviet history.

What Parts of the IB History Syllabus is This Guide Useful For?

1. Primarily, this guide is intended to help Higher and Standard Level candidates who are studying Lenin and/or Stalin's Russia as a case study for World History Topic 10: Authoritarian States for Paper 2.

2. In addition, it will be of help to Higher Level candidates who are studying Imperial Russia, revolution and the establishment of the Soviet Union (1855–1924) and The Soviet Union and post-Soviet Russia, as part of Higher Level Option 4: The History of Europe, syllabus sections 12 and 16 respectively.

Contents

Advice on Tackling Paper 2

What Do You Need to Know?

- The examination lasts **one and a half hours.**
- It is divided into **twelve** sections, each on a different world history topic.
- Authoritarian States (20th Century) is Topic 10.
- Two essay questions will be set on each topic, so twenty-four in total.
- Candidates have to answer **two** questions each chosen from **different** topics.
- The maximum mark for each question is 15.
- For Higher Level candidates, Paper 2 is worth 25% of the total assessment.
- For Standard Level candidates, Paper 2 is worth 45% of the assessment.
- The questions will be open (you can use your own examples); they will NOT refer to either named states or leaders.
- The IB syllabus specifies that the following aspects of authoritarian states should be studied:
  - The emergence of authoritarian states
  - Consolidation and maintenance of power
  - Aims and results of policies.
- Some questions will demand discussion of states from more than one region (there are four world regions as defined in the IBO handbook) and the IBO recommend that students study a minimum of three authoritarian states.

Advice on Tackling Essays

- You must spend a few minutes carefully looking at the paper and weighing up the choice of questions before you make up your mind on which two questions to answer.

- Look very closely at the wording of the questions, making sure that you understand their implications and what you need to address in your answer.

- Pay particular attention to 'command' words such as: 'to what extent', 'analyse', 'compare and contrast'. In the case of 'To what extent was any one authoritarian state you have studied a totalitarian state?' you must weigh up the ways in which the Soviet state was and the ways in which it was not totalitarian, reaching a conclusion about whether it was totally, largely, partly, or not at all, totalitarian. 'Compare and contrast the methods by which two leaders of authoritarian states came to power' would require you to examine the similarities and the differences between their methods. 'Analyse' means examine or scrutinise, so 'analyse the conditions which gave rise to an authoritarian state' would require you to examine the circumstances which made possible the Bolshevik Party's success, explaining which conditions (social, political, economic, military) benefited the Bolsheviks and evaluating which were most important.

- Always plan your answer, spending at least two or three minutes doing this for each essay, if not longer (but no more than five–six minutes).

- Give equal time to each essay you write. Do not be tempted to spend much longer on one at the expense of the other.

- Answer the question. Keep your approach analytical, do not drift into a description of events. Focus tightly on the question; do not deviate.

- Perhaps the best way of ensuring that each paragraph is linked to the title is to check that your first sentence (the 'key' sentence) is making a statement that directly answers the question.

- For each point that you make, provide an explanation of what light that point sheds on the question/why it is significant and also present evidence or a precise example to support it. So, the drill should be **'Statement, Explanation, Example'**.

- Always write in complete sentences and be as clear as you can in your use of English. The clearer your English, the more effectively you will communicate your points to the examiner.

- Always write a proper introduction. This must identify the key issues raised by the question. You should also outline your thesis, the line of argument that your answer will take.

- Make sure that you leave time for a proper conclusion. The main purpose of this is to restate your key arguments.

- Do not feel that you have to pack your answer with references to differing schools of historical interpretation and named historians. You will get credit for such historiographical references, where used appropriately, but do not insert them just for the sake of displaying your knowledge if they do not contribute to answering the question.

- Whatever information you insert into your answer, whether in the form of a fact, a statistic or a quotation, do make sure that you explain its significance and how it answers the question. If you do that, your essay should remain focused.

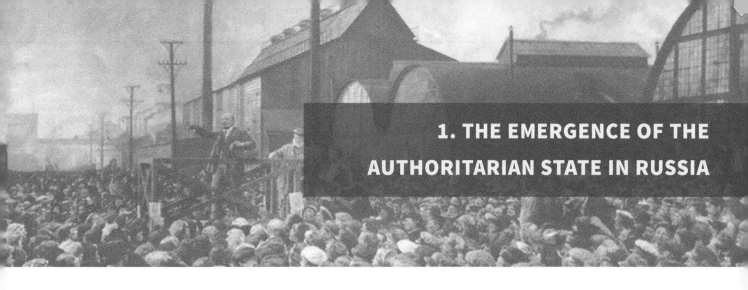

1. THE EMERGENCE OF THE AUTHORITARIAN STATE IN RUSSIA

TOPICS:
Long-term conditions
Short-term conditions
Methods

In October 1917, Lenin's **Bolshevik** Party seized power in Petrograd (known prior to the First World War as St Petersburg), the capital of Russia, and after a vicious Civil War, created the USSR (the Union of the Soviet Socialist Republics), a single party state which was to endure until 1991. In order to explain the success of the Bolsheviks in establishing the first socialist state in history, it is necessary to examine both the failings of the Russian monarchy, which collapsed in February 1917, and also of the short-lived **Provisional Government**, which filled the void left by the abdication of the last Tsar (emperor), Nicholas II. In addition, the Bolsheviks' strengths must be analysed, to determine how they successfully exploited conditions in order to overthrow the Provisional Government.

1.1 Long-term Conditions That Gave Rise to the Soviet State

The Russian Empire had been ruled by the Romanov dynasty since the 17th century and was a huge land mass, comprising of about fifty different nationalities. By the 19th century several fundamental weaknesses became apparent.

> **What long-term weaknesses of the Russian monarchy led to its collapse in 1917?**
>
> 1. A failure to match the military strength of European great powers such as Germany and France.
>
> 2. A failure to address widespread **peasant** poverty.
>
> 3. A failure to achieve the levels of industrialisation reached by western European governments, notably those of Britain and Germany.
>
> 4. An inability to broaden its political support through a programme of constitutional reform; Russia's monarchy was almost unique among the Great Powers in refusing (up to 1905) to share any of its power with its subjects.

> **What were the long-term military causes of the 1917 Revolutions?**
> At the beginning of the 19th century Russia had been one of the great military powers of Europe, which, under Tsar Alexander, had defeated Napoleon. However, over the course of the 19th century Russia fell far behind the other great powers, such as Britain and France,
>
> *(continued)*

 Author's Tip

Use these margins to write notes. There are also notes pages at the rear of this book.

 Key Terms

Bolshevik: the faction within the Russian Marxist movement led by Lenin; 'Bolshevik' means 'majority'. The Bolsheviks split from the 'Mensheviks' (meaning 'minority') in 1903.

Provisional Government: temporary government set up in March 1917 after Tsar Nicholas II abdicated; overthrown by the Bolsheviks in the October Revolution.

Peasant: either a farmer who owns or rents a very small amount of land or used to describe a labourer who works on a landowner's estate.

What were the long-term military causes of the 1917 Revolutions? *(continued)*

as the latter underwent profound economic and social changes due to rapid industrialisation. Russia's backwardness was cruelly exposed during the Crimean War (1854–1856) in which Tsar Nicholas I (1825–1855), and his son, Alexander II (1855–1881), saw Russia's armed forces humiliated on home soil by the British and French. Alexander II's Minister of War, Dmitri Miliutin, did introduce universal military service (1874) and the Russian Army performed rather better against Turkey in 1877–1878. However, Russia's lack of industrialisation meant that Russia was not in the same league in terms of military power as countries like Germany. This was highlighted by Russia's defeat by Japan in 1904–1905. A series of military reforms was instituted after this but they were not due for completion until 1917 and the outbreak of the First World War in 1914 caught Russia unprepared for a major conflict.

What were the long-term socio-economic causes of the 1917 revolutions?

1. Agricultural backwardness

Until the middle of the century, the bulk of the population was comprised of millions of serfs (peasants) who were tied to the land belonging to noble landlords and the Russian crown. In spite of Alexander II, the 'Tsar-liberator', granting them personal freedom in 1861, rural poverty remained a huge cause of social tension and peasant unrest grew in the last quarter of the 19th century and the opening years of the 20th.

The causes were:

- Chronic land shortage
- A rapidly growing peasant population
- Very low levels of literacy
- The burden of redemption payments that peasants were required to make in order to pay for the land they purchased from the landlords.

Peasant uprisings would play a major role in both the 1905 Revolution and the October 1917 Revolution.

2. Late but very rapid industrialisation

As noted above, little industrialisation took place in Russia before the 1890s. Although, the total number of industrial workers in Russia grew from 800,000 (1855) to about 1.3 million (1887), this was still only 1% of Russia's population (113 million) and Russia continued to fall further and further behind rapidly industrialising countries, notably the USA, Britain and Germany. It was not until the 1890s that the Russian government initiated a programme of rapid industrialisation in an attempt to catch up with the West and retain Russia's status as a great military power.

Coal production increased 500% in the years 1880 to 1900 to 16 million tons p.a. (per year). Russian industry grew at 8% p.a. in the 1890s and by 1900 had become the world's fifth industrial power, though still a long way behind Britain, France, Germany and the USA. However, industrial growth was highly dependent on foreign investment and a world recession from 1900 hit Russia hard, which was one of the causes of the 1905 Revolution.

Furthermore, both before and after the 1905 Revolution, the rapid pace of industrialisation caused huge strain on Russia as industrial workers crowded into the rapidly growing cities of St Petersburg and Moscow. The populations of St Petersburg and Moscow more than doubled in the period 1881-1914 (to 2.2 million and 1.3 million respectively).

The rapid pace of industrialisation did not just create immense social tensions in the towns, it also worsened the condition of the peasants because the peasants were being squeezed by high taxes which the government used to fund industrialisation. Higher levels of taxation meant that the peasants were obliged to sell more grain, therefore making them more vulnerable to famine. A series of bad harvests in the 1890s led to growing rural unrest.

What were the long-term political causes of the 1917 Revolutions?

The Tsarist monarchy was, until the 1905 Revolution, an **autocracy** under which political parties and organisations were illegal. As the 19th century wore on, it became apparent that growing sections of the educated classes felt alienated from the monarchy because of its refusal to share power with them. In this respect, Russia's political system failed to change when most other European monarchies were granting elected assemblies or devolving power more widely. Alexander II (1855-1881) did try to modernise Russia in certain respects; in addition to emancipation, he pushed through a whole series of educational, judicial, administrative and military reforms. However, he was intent on maintaining the autocratic power of the monarchy.

 Key Term

Autocracy: a system of government in which all political power is vested in one person.

1.1.1 The Development of Political Opposition

Paradoxically, opposition to the Tsarist system actually increased massively under the 'Tsar-liberator', partly because many of the educated classes had their hopes of fundamental change raised by Alexander's announcement that serfdom would have to be abolished, only to have them dashed by what they saw as a flawed reform which did not radically improve the lives of the Russian peasantry.

A variety of opposition groups emerged:

1. Liberals

The *zemstva* reform (1864), which introduced elected local councils, aroused hopes among Russian liberals of an elected **Duma**, which Alexander II then dashed. Historians see this as a tragedy since, after the assassination of Alexander II in 1881 by terrorists committed to a peasant revolution, it meant there was no chance for constitutional government to develop. Under Alexander II's son and grandson, Alexander III (1881–1894) and Nicholas II (1894–1917), the Russian monarchy followed a reactionary political course, resolutely opposed to sharing its power even with the educated classes. Instead, political reform was thrust upon an unwilling Nicholas II as a result of the 1905 revolution and so, arguably, was doomed to fail.

 Key Term

Liberals: individuals or groups committed to introducing an elected government along the lines of the British parliamentary system and who advocated safeguards for the liberties of the individual.

Duma: Russian word for 'parliament'.

2. Revolutionaries

From Alexander II's reign onwards two distinct types of revolutionary movement emerged within Russia. Whereas the liberals sought to pressurise the monarchy into conceding an elected assembly, revolutionaries sought the overthrow of the monarchy.

- Populists in the late 19th century and the **Social Revolutionaries (SRs)** in the early 20th century both aimed at a peasant revolution, which would see a huge transfer of land from the monarchy and nobility to the peasant masses. The Social Revolutionary Party was founded in 1901 and was led by Victor Chernov. The SRs campaigned for **universal suffrage** and a peasant revolution. They were involved in peasant risings in 1902 and their Combat Organisation organised terrorist attacks.

- The **Marxists**: from 1883 onwards, the ideas of the German communist writer, Karl Marx, began to attract growing numbers of Russian intellectuals who sought to transform Russia by means of a revolution of the industrial proletariat (factory workers). In 1898, the Russian Social Democratic Labour Party was established; Lenin was a founding member. However, the Russian Marxists proved very argumentative and remained divided throughout the period up to the 1917 Revolution, e.g. between the 'economists' who advocated pushing for better conditions for the industrial workers and those who argued for socialist revolution. In 1902, Lenin wrote *What Is To Be Done?* in which he argued for

 Key Term

Social Revolutionaries (SR): revolutionary party founded in Russia in 1901, dedicated to redistributing all land to the peasants and ending Tsarist rule.

Universal suffrage: voting rights for all adults.

Marxists: revolutionaries who adopted the ideas of Karl Marx and who sought to bring about a classless society.

Key Term

Vanguard: the advance guard of an army.

Key Term

Mensheviks: one of two main groups in to which the Russian Marxists split in 1903; the term means 'minority' in Russian.

the need for a disciplined, elite party of full-time revolutionaries to act as the '**vanguard**' of a proletarian revolution. The following year, the Social Democrats split over this issue when its leaders gathered for a congress at Brussels and London. Lenin's ideas were opposed by Julius Martov, who argued for a broad, less exclusive party; Lenin's faction became known as the Bolsheviks and Martov's as the **Mensheviks**. Before the outbreak of the First World War, both Marxist factions remained tiny in terms of membership and support.

1.1.2 The 1905 Revolution: Long-term Weaknesses of Tsarism Highlighted

The 1905 Revolution has often been presented as a dress rehearsal for the 1917 Revolutions because the long-term structural problems indicated above contributed to both the 1905 and 1917 Revolutions.

Causes

1. **Growing peasant unrest. This was the result of:**
   - High taxes (to pay for industrialisation)
   - Redemption dues (to pay for the land they acquired when they had been emancipated in 1861)
   - Overpopulation
   - Bad harvests from the late 1890s
   - Growing peasant literacy, partly the result of the 1874 military reform, meant peasant risings were more co-ordinated.

1902 onwards saw large-scale peasant revolts in the Ukraine; by 1904, there were risings across much of Russia. Peasants sought to increase their landholdings and lower their taxes, especially redemption dues.

2. **Industrial unrest**
   - Rapid industrial growth ended abruptly in 1899, largely because of an international financial crisis, which meant foreign investment dried up, but also because of bad harvests in 1897–1901, which led to a fall in government tax revenue.
   - The recession of 1900–1905 resulted in high unemployment and wage cuts.
   - There had been increasing numbers of strikes in the 1890s due to the terrible living and working conditions of the growing industrial **proletariat**. From the mid-1890s Marxist revolutionaries played a significant role in organising strikes.
   - Zubatov, Chief of Police in Moscow, organised official trade unions to try to channel working class discontent. This scheme backfired as the Zubatov unions organised large-scale strikes. In 1903 Father Gapon took up Zubatov's idea and in 1905 organised the protest which ended in the massacre of demonstrators by Tsarist troops known as 'Bloody Sunday'.

Key Term

Proletariat: marxist term for the industrial working class.

3. **Growing political opposition**
   - The Social Democratic Party was set up in 1898. This was a Marxist organisation.
   - The Social Revolutionary Party was set up in 1901 and aimed at peasant revolution.
   - The liberals were angered by military failures against Japan and formed the Union of Liberation which organised a series of reform banquets in 1904 but the Tsar only made vague promises of reform.

All of the above groups drew the majority of their leaders from the professional middle-classes who grew rapidly in numbers in the second half of the 19th century following Alexander II's reforms. The 1890s saw a revival of revolutionary and liberal opposition to the autocracy.

4. Growing unrest among many of the non-Russian peoples

This was in response to the Russification policies of Alexander III and Nicholas II, which involved imposing the Russian language and the Russian **Orthodox Church** on the Tsar's non-Russian subjects. Resentment was particularly great in Finland, which led to an upsurge in Finnish nationalism, including the assassination of Finland's governor-general, Bobrikov, in 1904.

5. Military disaster: the Russo-Japanese War (1904–1905)

Towards the end of the 19th century, Russia turned its attention to the Far East, encouraged by the weakness of the Chinese Empire. In 1898 the Chinese government allowed Russia the right to build a railway across Manchuria and a twenty-five year lease on the Liaotung Peninsula. Nicholas II's ministers looked to expand into Korea too, which brought Russia into conflict with Japan, which regarded Korea as within its sphere of influence. Japan attacked Russia's naval base in Manchuria, Port Arthur, in 1904.

Dec. 1904 — Port Arthur surrendered to the Japanese.

Feb. 1905 — The Russian army was defeated at Mukden.

May 1905 — Russia's Baltic fleet was destroyed in the Tsushima Straits.

Sep. 1905 — Russia agreed peace terms with Japan in the Treaty of Portsmouth; Russia had to withdraw from Manchuria.

6. Bloody Sunday: the trigger for revolution

In January 1905 demonstrators, led by Father Gapon, marched on the Winter Palace, carrying a petition. Troops killed probably over 1,000. This sparked a wave of strikes across Russia.

In July 1905, liberals set up the Kadet (Constitutional Democrats) Party, which was led by Paul Miliukov. They demanded an elected duma. By September, the country was in the grips of a general strike and there were widespread peasant rebellions and risings among some of the non-Russian nationalities. In October, the St Petersburg **Soviet** was set up to represent the interests of the workers. Trotsky was its chairman. It looked as if the monarchy might be overthrown. However, this was not to be the case.

How did the Russian monarchy survive the 1905 Revolution?
- Nicholas II reluctantly made concessions in the **October Manifesto**: he granted an elected state duma parliament and cancelled redemption payments. middle- and upper-class liberals were bought off by the manifesto. The October Manifesto also ensured the loyalty of the officer class and gave rise to a second liberal party, the Octobrists, who were committed to making the new parliamentary system work.
- The liberals were also prepared to support the government because they were worried by the establishment of the St Petersburg Soviet in October and the General Strike it organised. The working class and peasant revolutionaries were still dissatisfied as they had not won their demands for an 8-hour working day or for land redistribution.

Key Term

Orthodox Church: the eastern wing of the Christian church centred on Constantinople (modern-day Istanbul), which gradually split from Rome from the 8th century AD. Most Christians in Eastern Europe belong to the Orthodox Church, which in the Tsarist era was the official state church.

Key Term

Soviet: elected council.

Key Term

October Manifesto: the promises of political reform made by Nicholas II in October 1905.

Sep. 1905 — The Treaty of Portsmouth ended the war with Japan. Russian troops could now be moved back to Western Russia to restore order.

Dec. 1905 — The government arrested leading members of the St Petersburg Soviet and ruthlessly suppressed a workers' rising in Moscow.

April 1906 — Sergei Witte, the Prime Minister, negotiated a large loan from France, so Nicholas II's government was now financially more secure.
1906 saw an upturn in world trade and so the recovery of Russian industry. In 1906 Russian industry grew at a rate of 6%.

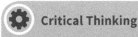

Critical Thinking

Was Tsarism doomed to fail by 1905? Was its survival until 1917 merely the postponement of the inevitable?

The Russian monarchy was lucky to survive the 1905 Revolution. It was weakened by terrible problems: rural unrest; backward agriculture; a discontented proletariat; and, alienated educated classes; restless nationalities.

The First World War destroyed the Russian monarchy but historians are divided over whether, if war had been avoided, reforms carried out in 1905–1914 might have provided the basis for its long-term survival. However, on balance, the evidence suggests that the monarchy was not adapting sufficiently to survive, particularly given the limitations of Nicholas II.

1.1.3 Reforms

Key Term

Non-commissioned officers: ranks, such as Corporal, below the officers and above the ordinary soldiers.

> **Overview**
> - The October Manifesto (1905) created the Duma.
> - Peter Stolypin's land reforms (1906–1911) permitted peasants to leave the *mir* (village communes).
> - Military reforms (1906 onwards): the establishment of a High Command; mobile artillery, the abolition of election of **non-commissioned officers (NCOs)**; and, more trains.

Constitutional reform

The October Manifesto provided Nicholas II with a great opportunity to win over the moderate educated classes,who were for so long alienated by the government's refusal to allow their participation in politics. The 1905 Revolution had demonstrated the disunity of the revolutionaries. The revolutionary movement was in decline after 1905; this was partly the result of 2,000 executions in 1906–1907.

Key Term

Veto: the power to block a law from being passed.

However, Nicholas II almost immediately undermined the October Manifesto with the Fundamental Laws (April 1906), under which Nicholas retained the right of **veto** over legislation and Ministers were responsible to him, not the Duma. The Tsar closed the first two dumas abruptly and then rigged the electoral system in 1907. Nicholas refused to work with the Duma, even in the case of the Third and Fourth Dumas where the more conservative Octobrists were the largest party. By 1914 the Duma parties were allying themselves with the growing strike movement. Nicholas' political incompetence undermined the monarchy's chances of survival, particularly once he became increasingly reliant on the self-styled holy man, Rasputin, whose unsavoury reputation undermined respect for the royal family.

Agricultural reform

Peter Stolypin (Prime Minister, 1906–1911) was banking on the 'sober and the strong'; he sought to encourage a prosperous peasant class by allowing peasants to consolidate their strips and leave the village commune. However,

- Only 20% of peasants broke away from the communes and agricultural productivity remained low.
- Only 5% of Russia's peasants were making a profit by 1914.
- Stolypin's reforms did not tackle the problem of rural overpopulation; Russia's population grew from 125 million in 1900 to 159 million by 1913. Even if the nobles' 140 million acres of land had been distributed among the peasantry, there would still have been land hunger.

Peasant unrest was a major factor in both the 1905 and 1917 revolutions. Stolypin had said that twenty years of peace were needed if Russia was to be stabilised; his reforms only had seven years of peace, but even before the First World War broke out the numbers of peasants leaving the communes had decreased.

Military reforms

Significant progress was made after the disastrous defeat against Japan in 1904–1905. This was shown by the relatively quick mobilisation at the start of the First World War in August 1914, which surprised the Germans. However, the military reforms were not due for completion until 1917. With Russia's army still far behind that of Germany, Nicholas II had to avoid war. However, humiliating diplomatic defeats in 1908–1909 and 1912–1913 during the crises over Austria-Hungary's annexation of Bosnia-Herzegovina and the Balkan Wars meant that the Russian government felt obliged to mobilise when Austria-Hungary attacked Serbia in July 1914. The First World War fatally undermined the loyalty of the Russian army and made revolution possible.

Industrialisation

- Russia's industrial proletariat (4.5 million by 1914) was concentrated in Kiev, Moscow and St Petersburg, living in awful conditions.
- Health Insurance, introduced in 1912, made little difference.
- 1906–1914 saw renewed industrial growth at a slightly less rapid rate than before 1900 (1906–1914 = average of 6% p.a.)
- There were relatively few strikes until 1912 when the Lena Massacre occurred in goldmines in Siberia; from then onwards there was a growing strike movement: 4,000 in the first six months of 1914.
- In spite of renewed industrialisation, Russia was still way behind the West; in 1914 Germany's coal production was five times that of Russia, its steel production four times that of Russia. Therefore, Russia faced a technologically superior Germany at the start of the First World War.

Why did the reforms of 1905–1914 prove 'too little and too late' to save the Russian monarchy?

- The Russian monarchy's problems proved too great to survive the immense strains imposed by the First World War.
- Rapid industrialisation and a backward agricultural system created huge tensions within Russia.
- Nicholas II's refusal to honour the spirit of the October Manifesto meant political support for the monarchy did not broaden.
- Amongst Nicholas II's Ministers, only Stolypin and Witte grasped the need for fundamental reform; Nicholas II dismissed Witte in 1905 and seemed to be on the point of dismissing Stolypin when he was assassinated in 1911.

1.2 Short-term Conditions That Gave Rise to the Soviet State in Russia

1.2.1 Short-term Causes of the 1917 Revolution

1. Military disaster in the First World War

Key Point

All of the long-term problems facing Tsarism were worsened by the impact of the First World War

"War is the locomotive of history" Leon Trotsky

Initially Russia's war effort got off to a promising start, with rapid mobilisation and Russian troops crossing into East Prussia (eastern Germany) within a few days of the outbreak of war. However, the German Army crushed the Russians at the Battles of Tannenburg and the Masurian Lakes. The Russian General Staff had only planned for a three month campaign, so supply problems became very serious. The Ministry of War had no plans for wartime production of munitions because it was assumed the reserve of 7 million shells was adequate.

Russia proved incapable of competing with Germany's armed forces because of the gulf between the two countries' industrial bases; Russia had only 4.5 million industrial workers out of a total population of 159 million. The government did recruit more factory workers but many of the new workers were untrained former peasants and therefore output actually fell at first. At the outbreak of war the Russian government failed to establish a Ministry of Supply. The generals, the Duma and industrial leaders had to put huge pressure on the government before it tackled the shell-shortage, and then this was not achieved until 1916.

May 1915

The First World War transformed an army of well-trained professional officers, commanding three year trained recruits into a colossal body of poorly trained conscripts; 9 million men were called up in the first twelve months. The Army expanded too quickly for sufficient numbers of officers to be trained and commissioned, so it was quite common for a regiment of 3,000 men to have no more than twelve officers. Therefore, there was a great reliance on NCO's who were largely drawn from the ranks of the peasantry. They became a radical group and were to lead the garrison mutinies of February 1917 and set up the Military Soviets. The Germans launched an offensive against Russia's North-West Front, resulting in the Germans occupying large areas of Western Russia. Consequently, General Brusilov withdrew Russian troops on the South-West Front. One million Russians surrendered in 1915.

Key Term

Petrograd: up until the First World War the Russian capital was known as St Petersburg but during the First World War, Nicholas II decided to rename it Petrograd because that is a Slavic name, whereas St Petersburg is a German place name. After Lenin's death in 1924, the Communist Party renamed Petrograd as Leningrad in honour of Lenin.

Aug. 1915

Nicholas II decided to appoint himself commander-in-chief, in spite of his Ministers' pleas for him not to. This proved disastrous as government became increasingly chaotic with the Tsar, based at Mogilev, hundreds of miles away from his Ministers and the Duma, in **Petrograd** (formerly St Petersburg). Furthermore, it gave greater authority to Tsarina Alexandra, who was widely unpopular because of her arrogance and German background, and to Rasputin,
who exerted a sinister influence over her and who now had a major say in ministerial appointments. Although Nicholas did not make the key military decisions, now that he was commander-in-chief, further defeats were blamed on him personally.

June 1916

General Brusilov launched a massive Russian offensive against the Austrians in Galicia. This, initially, proved a brilliant success but a German counter-offensive led to a major retreat by the Russians and a serious decline in morale among the Russian troops.

By 1917, 1.7 million Russians had been killed, 8 million wounded and 2.5 million were prisoners. The historian Norman Stone has shown that the Russian Army was not on the point of collapse in 1917 but morale was poor, the Germans had advanced deep into Western Russia, and the loss of many of the pre-war professional officers meant that discipline in the army was beginning to break down.

2. Economic Problems

a. Inflation: Government spending increased by 800% between 1914 and 1916. The Government printed more paper money and abandoned the gold standard. Prices increased by 400% between August 1914 and March 1917. The government made the sale of alcohol illegal and so lost much tax revenue because previously it had had a monopoly on the sale of vodka.

b. Food shortages: 15 million peasants were called up to the armed forces. Horses were requisitioned for the armed forces. Food shortages became very serious from 1916 when peasants started hoarding grain because they could not afford to buy scarce manufactured goods (at the now-inflated prices). The transport network focused on supplying the army's needs.

c. Crisis in the cities: The war worsened the problems already being caused by rapid industrialisation. Petrograd's population increased from 2.1 million to 2.65 million and Moscow's from 1.6 million to 2 million, leading to severe overcrowding. By 1917 state-owned factories were employing four times as many workers as in 1914 and 33% of these were in Petrograd. In 1917 less than 10% of factory workers received what was regarded as the minimum living wage of 200 roubles a month. Food shortages were worst in the cities. One million workers went on strike in 1916.

3. Political problems

Nicholas II continued to display a reluctance to work with the Duma, which particularly angered its members given the huge challenges that the war posed for Russia. In August 1914, the Duma voted money for the war, with only the Bolshevik deputies voting against. The Tsar then adjourned it and called the Duma back only for brief sessions in the following two and a half years.

The Duma politicians and other leading members of the middle and upper classes then proceeded to take their own measures to help the war effort as they became increasingly alarmed at the incompetence and lethargy of the Tsar's government. So essentially, an alternative government was beginning to evolve in Russia during the war years:

The Union of Zemstva, led by Prince Lvov, took over organising supplies and medical care; by 1916 it had 8,000 associated institutions. At first its work was supported by donations but eventually the government provided money.

The Central War Industries Committee was set up by leading industrialists in order to tackle the army's supply problems.

Nicholas recalled the Duma and most of the deputies (236/421) united to form the Progressive Bloc which demanded a *government of public confidence.* By this, they meant that the Tsar should choose his Ministers from the leading members of the largest parties in the Duma. It appears that a majority of the Tsar's Ministers advised him to make concessions to the Duma but Nicholas II did not and instead adjourned it again.

Nov. 1916 — Nicholas summoned another session of the Duma. The leader of the Kadets, Paul Miliukov, attacked government incompetence and posed the question whether this was the result of *"stupidity or treachery?"*

Dec. 1916 — Rasputin was murdered by Prince Yusupov but, even with Rasputin's malign influence removed, Nicholas II still opposed making political concessions. It is at this point that a group of Duma politicians, including the Octobrist and Kadet leaders, Miliukov and Guchkov, and the generals, Brusilov and Alexeyev, began to plot to remove the Tsar.

1.2.2 The February Revolution of 1917

Key Point

Old Style Dates: Up until the Bolshevik Revolution of 1917, Russia was using a calendar that the rest of Europe had abandoned a century or more before. Consequently, the Russian calendar was thirteen days behind that used in Western Europe. The Bolsheviks adopted the new calendar in February 1918, so from February 1918 onwards dates usually are shown in textbooks as 'New Style'. You may use either 'Old Style' or 'New Style' dates when writing about events in 1917, but do be consistent in doing so.

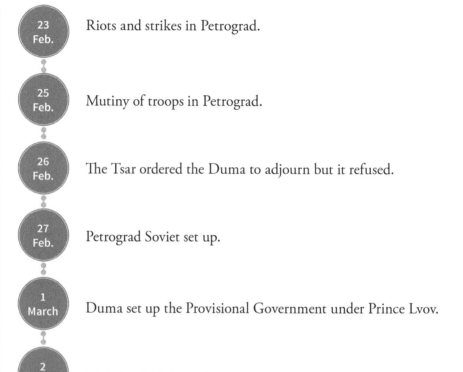

23 Feb. — Riots and strikes in Petrograd.

25 Feb. — Mutiny of troops in Petrograd.

26 Feb. — The Tsar ordered the Duma to adjourn but it refused.

27 Feb. — Petrograd Soviet set up.

1 March — Duma set up the Provisional Government under Prince Lvov.

2 March — Nicholas II abdicated.

The downfall of the Russian monarchy was not planned and took everyone by surprise, including revolutionary groups like the Bolsheviks. There were 400,000 workers in Petrograd and, by 23rd February, there were only nine days' supply of flour left. Demonstrations over bread shortages led to riots, which merged with a strike at the Putilov armaments factory. Unlike the 1905 Revolution, much of the Petrograd garrison openly sided with the rioters (the first mutinies occurred on 25th February) and the situation became serious.

26 Feb. — The Tsar's response was feeble, he was warned by both the military commander in Petrograd, General Khabalov, and by Rodzianko, the President of the Duma, but he did nothing. Worse still, on 26th February, Nicholas II dismissed the Duma.

27 Feb. — The Duma decided to continue to meet and on 27th February workers and soldiers marched on the Tauride Palace where the Duma was meeting. The Duma was unsure whether to support the rioters or not but one Socialist Revolutionary deputy, Alexander Kerensky, helped persuade them to do so. Rodzianko announced that the Duma was taking control of the capital. At the same time the workers and soldiers in Petrograd elected a Soviet as they had done during the 1905 Revolution.

By 28th February, most of the 160,000 soldiers in Petrograd had either mutinied or stopped trying to restore order. There were about 1,300 casualties in the fighting in Petrograd (half civilians, half soldiers and police). Rodzianko contacted General Alexeyev, Chief of the General Staff. They agreed that the Tsar's immediate abdication and the establishment of a new government were essential if order were to be restored.

Nicholas II, at Pskov, on his way back to the capital, was informed by his generals and a delegation of Duma deputies that they would no longer support him. Nicholas agreed to abdicate in favour of his son, Alexis, but later decided that he was too ill and so decided on his own younger brother, the Grand Duke Michael. Michael refused and so Russia became a republic.

The Duma leaders and generals had hoped to use the disturbances in Petrograd to force a change of Tsar, but had not intended to establish a republic. They had reached the conclusion that Nicholas II had to be removed if Russia were to stand any chance of winning the war and of avoiding a social revolution.

The Duma on 1st March chose ten of its members to serve as a Provisional Government; this was dominated by the liberal parties (Kadets and Octobrists). The Prime Minister was Prince Lvov, and the Provisional Government included one Socialist Revolutionary, Alexander Kerensky. Paul Miliukov was the Foreign Minister and Alexander Guchkov was Minister of War.

Whilst all of this was happening most of the leading Bolsheviks and Mensheviks were still in exile.

1.2.3 The October Revolution of 1917

The Failure of the Provisional Government (March–October 1917)

The simple answer to the question of why the Provisional Government fell after just eight months is that it was unable to resolve the problems that had caused the collapse of the monarchy.

What weakened the Provisional Government?

1. Its own reforms

The Provisional Government (PG) issued a series of liberal reforms, including freedom of the press, the release of political prisoners, and the abolition of the death penalty. It abolished the *Okhrana* (the Tsarist secret police). This reduced the government's coercive capabilities at a time of crisis, a dangerous move.

2. The Soviets: 'Dual Authority'

The PG intended to introduce a new, democratic system of local government but took until August to create a scheme. In the meantime, soviets (elected councils of workers, soldiers and peasants) had been set up across Russia to take charge of the localities. Therefore, the PG did not have effective control of Russia.

It used to be thought that the PG had responsibility but no power because of the existence of the Petrograd Soviet (PS) but historians now think that the PG had a window of opportunity in March-April when fear of a counter-revolution by conservative army officers bound the PS and PG together. However, it is difficult to see how the PG, which

(continued)

What weakened the Provisional Government? *(continued)*

essentially represented the propertied classes and was chosen by the Duma, and the PS, which primarily represented the working classes, could continue to work together in the long run.

On 1st March, the Soviet issued Order Number 1, which required all army units to elect soldiers' committees and said that soldiers should only obey the PG if its orders had been approved by the PS.

3. Continuing defeats in the war

The PG and PS were both in favour of continuing the war but had different attitudes to it. Miliukov and the PG were strongly committed to the war, the propertied classes were, largely, very nationalistic and sought territorial gains from the war (e.g. Constantinople from Turkey). The PG was also heavily dependent on loans from its allies. The Soviets argued in favour of 'revolutionary defencism', that is a war of self-defence or a war against German imperialism.

In April, Miliukov sent a secret note to the Allies saying that the PG did not agree with the Soviets' call for the rejection of imperialist war aims by all the warring nations. This note was made public and provoked riots in Petrograd. Miliukov and Guchkov resigned and six Socialists joined the PG in May.

Alexander Kerensky now became War Minister and organised a massive offensive in June 1917; by the first week in July this had failed disastrously, with 1 million casualties. News of this provoked serious disturbances in Petrograd known as the July Days. During the late summer and autumn of 1917, desertion became widespread among soldiers and military discipline began to breakdown.

4. Peasant land seizures

The PG accepted the need for land redistribution but insisted that this could only be carried out with compensation to the noble landowners (the PG represented the propertied classes) and would have to wait until a Constituent Assembly met (and it kept on postponing elections for the Constituent Assembly). The peasants were not prepared to wait and by September there was a growing number of land seizures, with the peasant soviets deciding on how the land should be redistributed. These seizures provoked growing desertions among the armed forces and further reduced food supplies as the estates being seized and broken up were often the most efficient ones.

1.3 Methods Used to Establish an Authoritarian State

1.3.1 How the Bolsheviks were able to seize power in October 1917

i. Lenin persuaded the Bolshevik Party that a second revolution was possible

 Key Term

April Theses: name given to the ideas that Lenin put forward on his return to Russia from exile in April 1917. Essentially, he urged his supporters to prepare for a second revolution.

When Nicholas II abdicated, Lenin was in exile in Switzerland. The German government, intent on destabilising Russia, arranged for Lenin's return to Russia in a sealed train in April 1917. On 4th April, Lenin delivered his *April Theses* in which he argued that the Soviets had the sole right to govern. Lenin said that the task of the Bolsheviks was not to extend freedom to all classes but to transfer power to the working classes. Most Bolsheviks had, like the Mensheviks and Socialist Revolutionaries, believed that they should support the PG in order to prevent a right-wing counter-revolution, convinced that a proletarian revolution was impossible in Russia given the small size of its industrial working class. It took several weeks before Lenin was able to win over the rest of his party to the idea of a second revolution.

Peace, Bread, Land, all power to the Soviets

In the April Theses, Lenin coined the slogan *"Peace, Bread, Land, all power to the Soviets"*. This proved in the long-term very attractive to ordinary Russians, particularly urban workers and garrison soldiers, who became desperate to see an end to the war, high inflation and food shortages.

However, until autumn 1917 it was the Mensheviks and Socialist Revolutionaries who dominated the Soviets and not the Bolsheviks.

In June 1917, when the First All-Russian Congress of Soviets met, the Bolsheviks won only 12% of the seats.

Distribution of seats in the First All-Russian Congress of Soviets	
SRs	285
Mensheviks	245
Bolsheviks	105

ii. Lenin's policy of opposing the PG meant that as the latter became more unpopular, the Bolsheviks increased their support

All of the other major parties, including the Social Revolutionaries and the Mensheviks, supported and indeed participated in the PG. As the PG grew increasingly unpopular, the Bolsheviks, who alone unreservedly opposed the PG, picked up more support. In February 1917, the Bolsheviks probably had in the region of 10,000 members; by October, this had grown to around 300,000 and most of them were concentrated in Petrograd and Moscow.

iii. The Bolsheviks were able to survive the setback they suffered during the July Days

News of the failure of Kerensky's Offensive sparked a rebellion in Petrograd, known as the July Days. It is difficult to know who was responsible for the July Days (3rd-6th July). Afterwards the Bolsheviks said the SRs and Mensheviks had begun the rising, whereas the SRs and Mensheviks blamed the Bolsheviks. It is probable that the workers of Petrograd and sailors from the nearby Kronstadt naval base started the rising and then called on the Bolsheviks to take a lead. At this stage the PG still had sufficient military support and was able to restore order by bringing up loyal troops from the front.

Kerensky now became Prime Minister and arrested a number of leading Bolsheviks, branding them as German agents. Lenin went into hiding. Kerensky brought in more Socialists as members of the PG but the PG was still dominated by its four Kadet members.

iv. Lenin revised Karl Marx's line on the peasants

Marx had dismissed the peasants as incapable of acting as a revolutionary class. Lenin adjusted this view because the peasants made up 80% of the Russian population and were war-weary and already seizing land. Lenin argued that Russian circumstances were such that the peasants could be a genuinely revolutionary force. The Bolsheviks did not have their own land policy so they simply adopted that of the SRs and accepted peasant land seizures. This won some peasant support for the Bolsheviks and led to some SRs being prepared to support the Bolsheviks (they became known as the Left SRs).

v. The Kornilov Affair in August 1917 boosted support for the Bolsheviks

This episode enabled the Bolsheviks to recover from their setback in the July Days. General Kornilov was the commander of the Russian forces on the South-West Front. He believed that it was necessary to destroy revolutionary forces in Russia before Russia could defeat Germany:

> It's time to hang the German supporters and spies, with Lenin at their head, and to disperse the Soviet.

Kornilov told Kerensky that he intended to bring loyal troops to Petrograd to restore order. It is not clear whether Kerensky first approved of this but then changed his mind when he suspected Kornilov intended to set up a dictatorship, or if it was just Kornilov's plan.

Kerensky, short of loyal troops in the capital, released Bolsheviks from prison and armed the Petrograd workers, many of them Bolshevik supporters. These militias were known as the '**Red Guards**'. In the end, Kornilov's advance did not reach Petrograd as railway workers sabotaged the railway tracks and some of Kornilov's troops mutinied. Kornilov was arrested. The Kornilov affair exposed the weakness of the PG and bolstered support for the Bolsheviks in Petrograd.

> **Key Term**
>
> **Red Guards:** armed groups of Bolshevik supporters, largely drawn from the working classes.

vi. The Bolsheviks gained majorities in the Petrograd and Moscow Soviets in September 1917

In mid-September, the Bolsheviks achieved majorities in the Petrograd and Moscow Soviets. This was to some extent because the other parties were less committed than the Bolsheviks at attending meetings of the Soviets and their sub-committees. In March 1917, 3,000 deputies had gathered for the first meeting of the PS. By autumn 1917, attendance was just a few hundred. More importantly, as the authority of the PG crumbled, it was the Bolsheviks who benefited most in terms of increased support, as it was they who were implacably opposed to it and appeared to offer to the workers and garrison soldiers a genuine alternative to the PG's policies.

vii. The Provisional Government's authority was undermined by the mushrooming of grassroots organisations:

- The spread of the Soviets
- The increasing number of factory committees elected by the workers to run the factories
- Growing land seizures by the peasants
- The creation of independent national governments, e.g. in the Ukraine.

After the Kornilov Affair the Soviets moved increasingly to the Left and the PG increasingly to the Right. A clash, therefore, was increasingly likely.

As Lenin put it:

> Either a soviet government or Kornilovism. There is no middle course.

On 12th September, Lenin urged the Bolsheviks to prepare for immediate revolution. He was worried about the outcome of the elections to the Second All-Russian Congress of Soviets, due to meet late October, and the elections for the Constituent Assembly due in November. He was convinced that the Bolsheviks had to seize control before these elections because both might go against the Bolsheviks.

viii. Lenin was able to persuade doubters among the Bolshevik leadership that the time was right to stage a second revolution

The Central Committee of the Bolshevik Party remained dubious about an immediate revolution, and some leading Bolsheviks opposed the idea of a Bolshevik takeover, preferring to see a coalition of socialist parties—Bolsheviks, Mensheviks, SRs—taking power. On 7th October, Lenin slipped back into Petrograd and, on 10th October, the Central Committee agreed in principle on staging a revolution but it did not decide on a date. Ironically it was the PG which determined the date of the Bolshevik revolution as Kerensky, fearing a rising, ordered the arrest of leading Bolsheviks and the closing down of their newspapers on 23rd October. Lenin ordered an immediate rising.

ix. Trotsky used Bolshevik control of the Petrograd Soviet to plan and stage the seizure of Petrograd

Leon Trotsky, who had joined the Bolsheviks in July 1917, having previously been a Menshevik, organised the Bolshevik rising, using his positions as Chairman of the Petrograd Soviet and Chairman of the Soviet's Military Revolutionary Committee.

1.3.2 The October Revolution

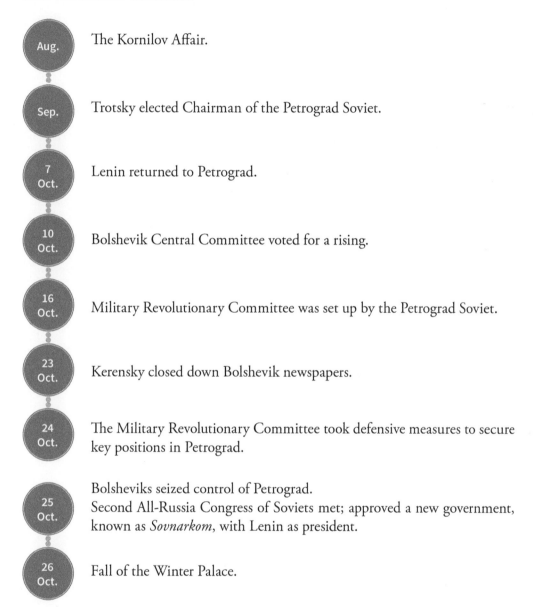

Aug. The Kornilov Affair.

Sep. Trotsky elected Chairman of the Petrograd Soviet.

7 Oct. Lenin returned to Petrograd.

10 Oct. Bolshevik Central Committee voted for a rising.

16 Oct. Military Revolutionary Committee was set up by the Petrograd Soviet.

23 Oct. Kerensky closed down Bolshevik newspapers.

24 Oct. The Military Revolutionary Committee took defensive measures to secure key positions in Petrograd.

25 Oct. Bolsheviks seized control of Petrograd.
Second All-Russia Congress of Soviets met; approved a new government, known as *Sovnarkom*, with Lenin as president.

26 Oct. Fall of the Winter Palace.

The revolution took place between late on 24th October and 26th October. Trotsky called on the garrison of the Peter and Paul Fortress to take control of the city in the name of the Soviets. There was little fighting and perhaps only five people were killed during the takeover. The PG had very few loyal troops left: a few officer cadets, a women's battalion and a bicycle regiment. Most of the soldiers in Petrograd and the sailors from the nearby naval base at Kronstadt supported the Bolshevik rising. While Kerensky managed to escape, the rest of the PG was arrested when the Winter Palace was taken early on 26th October.

On the evening of 25th October, the Second All-Russian Congress of Soviets met. Despite Lenin's earlier misgivings, the Bolsheviks had over 300 delegates out of a total of 649 and Lenin informed the delegates that the PS had seized power in their name. The Right SRs and Mensheviks walked out in protest, but the Left SRs were prepared to support the Bolsheviks.

1.3.3 Key Historical Perspectives: The October Revolution

The official Communist Party view
- The October Revolution was the inevitable result of class struggle.
- They stress the brilliance of Lenin's leadership.
- It was a popular revolution, inspired and organised by the Bolshevik Party.

The Liberal view (e.g. Robert Conquest, Richard Pipes)
- Ruthless Bolsheviks took advantage of the collapse of government authority to seize power.
- The October Revolution was a **coup d'etat** by the Bolsheviks who had only limited popular support.
- The Bolsheviks were successful because of their organisational skills and the leadership of Lenin and Trotsky.

Revisionist views (e.g. Orlando Figes)
- They emphasise the importance of revolution from below. Revisionists argue that there was a growing popular movement, characterised by the growing influence of the Soviets, in Russia that would have overthrown the Provisional Government without the Bolsheviks' intervention.
- The Bolsheviks exploited this popular revolution to their advantage and betrayed the people by imposing a brutal single-party dictatorship, suppressing the workers' movement.

 Key Term

Coup d'etat: the seizure of power by force.

TOPICS:
Decrees and measures
The Civil War
Single party rule
The nature of the party and the state

The Bolsheviks were in control of Petrograd as a result of their insurrection on 24th October but elsewhere the Bolshevik take-over was not so smooth. Fighting lasted a week in Moscow between officers and Red Guards, with 500 killed. It was the end of November before other cities were won over. Rural areas were much more difficult to deal with and very few peasants were Bolshevik supporters. Civil war did not break out at this stage, partly because the Bolsheviks' opponents were waiting to see what would happen when elections to the Constituent Assembly were held on 12th November. Most people did not expect the new government to last long because of the scale of the problems it would face:

1. Economic crisis; by November 1917 prices were 1,000% higher than they had been in 1914.

2. Opposition from other political groups.

3. The War; by late 1917, the Germans had advanced closer to Petrograd.

Lenin was more realistic than many of the Bolsheviks: he realised that the Bolsheviks would have to fight a civil war to gain control of the rest of Russia, and that this would involve ignoring many of the principles of communism and creating a ruthless, dictatorial government. In December 1917, Lenin set up the Cheka, the Bolshevik secret police. Lenin also believed that the Communist revolution could not survive in Russia alone, but must be spread to other, more industrialised countries.

2.1 Bolshevik Decrees and Measures

At the end of October, Sovnarkom published a series of decrees and measures (which did not strictly reflect Bolshevik ideology but were an attempt to satisfy the Russian masses):

1. The Decree on Land

This decree handed over the estates of the crown, church and aristocracy to the peasants. This effectively legalised what the peasants had already done. Some Bolsheviks were very angry about this because they believed that, since land was part of the means of production, it should now belong to the state, not to individual peasants. However, Lenin's pragmatic view was accepted because 300,000 Bolsheviks could not deprive 125 million peasants of their land. In February 1918, the Bolshevik government passed a decree declaring that all land belonged to the state, but did not attempt to implement it.

2. The Decree on Workers' Control of the Factories

Again, the Bolsheviks pragmatically recognised what had already happened, that the industrial workers had seized control of the factories, even though many of the factory committees were controlled by the Mensheviks.

3. State Capitalism

This is the term used to describe the economic policy of the Bolsheviks from October 1917 to June 1918, when War Communism replaced it. Bolshevik economic policy during this period, and throughout the Civil War, was improvised. Lenin's economic writings before 1917 had been very theoretical, he had given little thought to economic planning. Therefore, from 1917 to summer 1918 the Bolsheviks had to use existing economic structures; in December, they did establish *Vesenkha* (the Supreme Council of the National Economy) to regulate the national economy, but its control was limited at first. However, it did nationalise banks and railways and cancelled debts owed to foreign governments.

4. The Decree on Nationalities

The Bolsheviks declared that the non-Russian peoples had the right to break away from the former Russian Empire. Independence movements had already sprung up in a number of areas, notably the Ukraine, Georgia, and the Baltic region. The Bolsheviks would later use the Red Army to force the Ukraine and Georgia into the USSR (the Union of Soviet Socialist Republics, formally set up in 1922).

5. The Decree on Peace

On 25th October (8th November 'New Style'), the Bolsheviks published a decree calling for a 'just, democratic peace' between all countries involved in the war. Lenin seems to have regarded his call for a peace settlement without land transfers and reparations as a public relations' exercise, because he knew that the priority was to achieve a quick peace settlement if the Bolsheviks were to consolidate their power and that would mean accepting harsh terms from Germany.

Key Term

Commissar: the name given by the Bolsheviks to Government Ministers.

Trotsky, the **Commissar** for Foreign Affairs, favoured trying to spin the peace talks out in the hope that, when the German workers saw how greedy their government was for land given the growing burdens imposed by the war on the German population, they would revolt and Germany would have its own communist revolution. Peace talks opened at Brest-Litovsk in December 1917.

An armistice (ceasefire) was agreed for 22nd November and peace talks began at Brest-Litovsk in December 1917. Trotsky's delaying tactics—'neither peace, nor war'—only irritated the Germans who launched a new offensive against the Russians in February 1918. Lenin insisted that a treaty must be signed and, in spite of opposition from several leading Bolsheviks including Trotsky and Bukharin, the Bolshevik government agreed. Trotsky resigned as Commissar for Foreign Affairs, but remained Commissar for War.

Key Point

Change of capital to Moscow: the Communist Party decided in March 1918 to make Moscow the capital of Russia instead of Petrograd.

6. The Treaty of Brest-Litovsk (March 1918)

As a result of the terms of the treaty that Germany imposed on Russia, Russia lost one third of its population and one third of its arable land. Some of the key terms were:

- Russia lost Poland, Estonia, Latvia, Lithuania, Finland, the Ukraine and Georgia.
- Russia had to pay an indemnity of 6,000 million marks.

Russia regained the Ukraine and Georgia in 1921 and, after Germany's defeat in 1918, the Baltic states (Latvia, Lithuania, and Estonia) and Poland were given their independence.

Lenin favoured accepting the German demands because Russia was too weak to continue the war, and only by making peace could the Bolsheviks concentrate on consolidating and extending their control within Russia and sorting out the economic problems that had brought about the downfall of both the Tsar and the Provisional Government. In any case, Lenin believed that ultimately workers revolutions would break out in Germany and other European countries and that any losses of territory would be temporary. His perspective, therefore, was not that of a Russian nationalist but of an international socialist.

The Left Social Revolutionaries, who had supported the Bolsheviks since the October Revolution, now resigned in protest from *Sovnarkom*, meaning that the Bolsheviks held every position in it. On 8th March, the Seventh Congress of the Bolshevik Party changed the name of the party to the **Communist Party** and, on 10th March, Lenin moved the capital from Petrograd to Moscow.

7. Elections to the Constituent Assembly (November 1917)

The Bolsheviks had criticised the Provisional Government for delaying elections to the Constituent Assembly and some Bolsheviks favoured a broad coalition of socialist parties, so Lenin felt that he had to allow elections to go ahead on 12th November. He correctly anticipated that the Bolsheviks would not do well:

Party	Number of seats in the Constituent Assembly
Bolsheviks	175 (24%)
Left SRs	40
Right SRs	370 (52%)
Mensheviks	16
Kadets	17
National Parties	86

 Key Term

Communist Party: the Bolshevik Party officially changed its name to 'Communist Party' in March 1918.

8. Lenin's closure of the Constituent Assembly (January 1918)

On 5th January, the Constituent Assembly met and elected the leader of the Right SRs, Victor Chernov, as its President. The Bolsheviks, who were in the minority, withdrew and Lenin sent in the Red Guards to close down the Assembly. On 6th January, Lenin declared that the Assembly was permanently dissolved. Lenin was opposed to Western ideas of democracy, believing in the need for a dictatorship of the Bolshevik Party to rule on behalf of the working classes.

Trotsky remarked that:

> "We have trampled underfoot the principles of democracy for the sake of the loftier principles of a social revolution."

Lenin's actions were criticised by foreign communists such as the German leaders Rosa Luxemburg and Karl Liebknecht. It led to a civil war within Russia that would last until late 1920, ending in Bolshevik victory and transforming the Bolshevik Party itself.

9. The establishment of a secret police

The Bolsheviks set up the *Cheka*, a secret police force, in December 1917. The *Cheka* was led by Felix Dzerzhinsky.

2.2 The Civil War (1918–1920)

By the spring of 1918, armed opposition to the Bolsheviks emerged in many parts of Russia.

The Whites

Key Term

Whites: the opponents of the Communists in the Civil War became known as the 'Whites'. White is a colour traditionally associated with monarchy.

The anti-Bolsheviks, known as the **Whites**, consisted of very diverse groups including ex-Tsarist commanders, Kadets, and right-wing political organisations. Many army commanders were anti-communist who, now Russia had pulled out of the First World War, could attempt to overthrow the Bolsheviks. They included:

- General Kornilov and General Denikin, who led an anti-Bolshevik army in the South
- Admiral Kolchak who commanded anti-Bolshevik forces in Western Siberia and became the most important White leader
- General Yudenich who led a White army in Estonia.

The SRs and Mensheviks

Key Term

Reds: The Communists in the Civil War became known as the 'Reds'. Red is a colour traditionally associated with revolution and radicalism.

For much of 1918, the Social Revolutionaries fought against the Communists (**Reds**). In June 1918, the Executive Committee of the Soviets expelled all Right Social Revolutionaries and Mensheviks from the Soviets for openly attacking the Communist (Bolshevik) dictatorship and the Treaty of Brest-Litovsk. The Left Social Revolutionaries had already resigned from *Sovnarkom* over the terms of the Treaty of Brest-Litovsk.

In July, the SRs unsuccessfully attempted to seize power in Moscow. The Communists (Bolsheviks) now expelled the Left SRs from the Soviets. In August, an SR assassin, Fanny Kaplan, seriously wounded Lenin. In June 1918, Victor Chernov set up an SR government in Samara. However, Admiral Kolchak, the White leader east of the Urals, soon clashed with the SRs. The Communists relaxed their persecution of the SRs and Mensheviks in November 1918 and many of the SRs and Mensheviks then fought on the Communists' side.

The Greens

Also fighting in the Civil War, against both the Communists (Reds) and the Whites, were the Greens. These were peasant forces, the largest of which were in the Ukraine led by the anarchist Nestor Makhno. In addition, nationalist movements in the Baltic, Ukraine, and Georgia were trying to break away from Russian control. In the case of Georgia, a popular Menshevik government remained in power until the Red Army overthrew it in 1921.

Red and White Terror

Both the Reds and the Whites resorted to Terror as a means of destroying opposition and intimidating the population into obedience. The Red Terror formally began in September 1918, but it had unofficially existed since July. During the Civil War, the *Cheka* executed at least 50,000 people.

The start of the Civil War is difficult to date exactly but is often identified with the revolt of the Czech Legion in May 1918. The Czech Legion were Austro-Hungarian prisoners of war who were returning, via the Trans-Siberian Railway, to Western Europe to fight against the Central Powers in the hope of setting up an independent Czech state. They clashed with Bolshevik troops in May and decided to join with the Whites against the Bolsheviks.

Foreign intervention

The Whites received help from the USA, Britain, France, Italy, and Japan. However, this help was half-hearted and soon withdrawn.

The interventionist powers were:

- Worried about the possibility of a communist revolution spreading to their own countries
- Angry that the Bolsheviks refused to pay back foreign loans
- Initially hoped that, if they helped overthrow the Bolsheviks, Russia might come back into the war against Germany.

British intervention did help ensure that the Baltic states were able to break away from Russia and become independent.

2.2.1 The Course of the Civil War

The initial phase was marked by gains for the Whites. The Czech Legion attacked the Bolsheviks. Foreign powers began to send troops to Russia in June.

The Bolsheviks counter-attacked against the Czechs and recaptured Kazan (about 300 miles east of Moscow). In November, Admiral Kolchak took control of the White forces in the east.

This was the most dangerous period for the Bolsheviks because they faced White offensives, launched by Kolchak in March, Denikin in August-October, and Yudenich in September-October. By October, the situation looked very threatening for the Bolsheviks and Lenin proposed withdrawing from Petrograd (Trotsky persuaded the Bolshevik Central Committee against this). However, White offensives were not co-coordinated and Trotsky, as War Commissar, was able to deal with them separately. The foreign powers began to withdraw their forces; most were gone by December.

Admiral Kolchak was captured and executed. The last White army was evacuated from the Crimea in December 1920.

2.2.2 War with Poland (1920–1921)

In January 1920, the Reds recaptured the Ukraine but the Polish government then invaded the Ukraine in an attempt to expand its borders.

In July the Red commander, General Tukhachevsky, forced the Poles out of the Ukraine and invaded Poland. Lenin expected the Polish workers to rise in revolt against the Polish government but they did not and the Red army was driven back into Russia.

In October, an armistice was signed, leading to the Treaty of Riga (March 1921).

> **Why did the Reds (Communists) win the Civil War?**
> **1. The Whites lacked political unity or unified leadership**
> They were weakened by the fact that they had diverse aims: some wanted to restore the Tsar, others to set up a moderate republic or a military dictatorship. The murder of the royal family at Ekaterinburg in July 1918 removed the possibility that the Whites might rally around them.
> *(continued)*

Why did the Reds (Communists) win the Civil War? *(continued)*

2. The Whites never co-ordinated their attacks

White forces, spread out over thousands of miles, failed to link up; the nearer to Moscow they got, the more strained their lines of communication became.

3. The Communists were more united and had better leadership

In contrast to the Whites, the Communist Party was united behind Lenin and had a shared ideology (Marxism). Lenin and Trotsky were very effective leaders; they were ruthless and pragmatic. Lenin was able to push through controversial yet necessary policies such as reintroducing management of factories by one manager and employing ex-Tsarist officers in the Red Army.

4. The Communists controlled a more coherent and compact area

The Communists were defending a central region well served by railways and their lines of communication were much shorter than those of the Whites. The Communists controlled the great industrial centres of Moscow and Petrograd.

5. Trotsky, as War Commissar, formed the Red Army and made it into a disciplined force

- Trotsky and Lenin rejected the demands of some leading Communists that the Party adopt Revolutionary Warfare. Lenin and Trotsky resorted to conscription in May 1918, instead of relying on the ill-disciplined but enthusiastic Red Guard militias that had been formed in 1917. By the end of 1918 the Red Army was 100,000 strong; by April 1919, 500,000; and by June 1920, 5 million. By contrast, the Whites never managed to raise more than 650,000 soldiers.

- In the face of bitter opposition from other leading Communists, Trotsky recruited 50,000 former Tsarist officers. Trotsky said that the officers were "to be squeezed like lemons and discarded later." Former officers who refused to serve were put into concentration camps and the families of those who did agree to fight were held hostage to ensure the officers' loyalty.

- The Communist Party appointed political commissars to every army unit; Trotsky described the commissars as the "iron corset". Trotsky toured the fronts in an armoured train and dealt mercilessly with deserters and incompetents.

- Trotsky restored the practice of appointing, rather than electing, officers.

6. Lenin was able to present the Bolsheviks as a patriotic government fighting against foreigners

The Whites were unpopular because of their foreign support and their brutality (though the Bolsheviks were as brutal).

7. Foreign support for the Whites was limited and was withdrawn by the end of 1920

8. The peasants hated the Whites

This was because the Whites were committed to restoring land to the nobility.

9. From May 1918, Lenin took measures to control the economy, which were known as War Communism

These were, however, only partly successful.

 Critical Thinking

What were the key features of the Red Army?

Key features of War Communism

- All factories of any size were nationalised and military discipline was applied to the factories.
- Middle class managers, accountants, and engineers were brought back to run the factories, most of which had been placed under workers' control in the months after the revolution, usually with disastrous results.

(continued)

Key features of War Communism *(continued)*

- Food and grain were seized from the peasants by Red Guards in order to feed the workers and the troops.
- The old inflation-ridden currency was abandoned. Instead wages were paid in food and fuel and trade was by barter.

What were the results of War Communism?

- The peasants decided it was not worth growing food for the Communists to take and so reduced their sowing. The result was a terrible food shortage, leading to possibly 7,500,000 deaths.
- Food shortages in the towns led to large-scale migration from the cities; between 1917 and 1920 the urban population fell by 33%.
- War Communism did not prevent a continuing fall in industrial and agricultural output; by 1921 the grain harvest was only 50% of the 1913 level and industrial production had fallen to just 20% of the 1913 level. However, the economic crisis was just as bad in the areas controlled by the Whites.
- War Communism ensured that the Red Army was fed and equipped. It took the majority of resources: e.g. 60% of food, and 70% of shoes.

2.2.3 The Consequences of the Civil War and of the Communists' Victory

The Communist government had survived the Civil War but its ruthless methods had made it deeply unpopular. When Lenin had been planning the 1917 Revolution, he had assumed that revolution would spread to other parts of Europe, but, by 1921, Lenin realised that Russia would be the only country with a Communist government for some time. Communist revolutions had failed in Germany and Hungary in 1919–1920. Lenin, therefore, knew that he would need both a strong army and secret police to defend his government from external and internal threats. The 'dictatorship of the proletariat', or more accurately the dictatorship of the Communist Party, would have to continue indefinitely.

Crises facing the Communist Party in 1921

1. The Krondstadt Rebellion (February-March 1921)

In February-March 1921, sailors at the naval base at Kronstadt, near Petrograd, revolted against the Communist Party, claiming that the Communists had broken all the promises that they had made to the Russian people and that the *Cheka* was arresting members of other socialist parties and stealing the peasants' crops. Eventually the rising was crushed by the Red Army, with a huge loss of life. The rebellion alarmed the Communist leadership because the Kronstadt sailors had been among their most committed supporters in 1917 and during the Civil War.

2. Rebellion in Tambov Province

Peasants in Tambov rebelled and attacked and robbed grain convoys.

3. Widespread strikes

Strikes occurred in 77% of Russia's large and medium-sized factories during 1920.

4. Economic chaos and famine

Agricultural and industrial output had fallen drastically as a result of the Civil War and the losses incurred under the Treaty of Brest-Litovsk. In excess of 7 million Russians died of famine and disease in 1921, leading Lenin to call on the International Red Cross for help.

2.3 The Establishment of Single Party Rule

Ever since the closure of the Constituent Assembly in January 1918, it had been apparent that Lenin had no intention of sharing power with any other parties. For the majority of the Civil War many Mensheviks and Socialist Revolutionaries had fought in the Red Army but in 1921, with the Communists victorious, Lenin banned the Menshevik and Socialist Revolutionary parties, making the Communist Party the sole legal party in the Soviet Union. In the same year, Lenin expelled 150,000 members of the Communist Party, mostly former Mensheviks and Socialist Revolutionaries.

2.3.1 The Creation of the Union of Soviet Socialist Republics (USSR)

Lenin had promised that the various nationalities of the Tsar's former empire would be allowed to choose whether they wished to be part of Russia or to be independent. Once Lenin was assured of victory in the Civil War, he reneged on this promise; as the Red Army captured areas during the Civil War, they imposed Communist governments on them and turned them into Soviet Socialist Republics. In 1923, a new constitution created the Union of Soviet Socialist Republics (USSR). Each Republic had its own government, which, in theory, could make decisions in certain areas of policy, such as health and education, without reference to Moscow. In economic policy, the Republics acted under the instructions of local Commissars who followed orders from a Union Commissar in Moscow. Foreign and Defence policy were entirely directed from Moscow by all Union-Commissars.

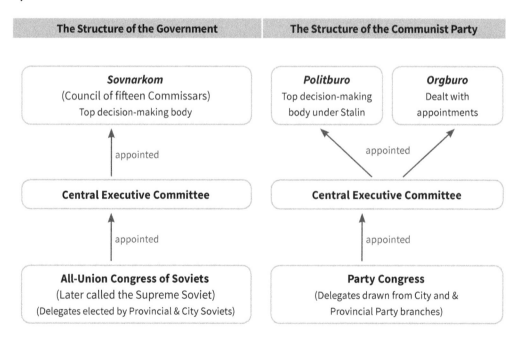

2.4 The Nature of the Party and the State in the USSR

1. Hierarchies in Party & State

Both the Party and State organisations were organised in a hierarchical pyramid (see diagram above). In theory, power flowed from the base (local Party branches and local Soviets), but in practice power flowed from the top downwards. The Party followed the principle of *'Democratic Centralism'* which meant that the leadership was elected but that once policy-decisions had been made they were binding on the Party members. Increasingly, decision-making was monopolised at the top of the state and party structures.

2. The Party was the principal organisation in the USSR, dominating state institutions

Membership of *Sovnarkom* (the Cabinet), the highest state institution, was monopolised by the Communist Party leadership. In turn, local state institutions, the Soviets, met less and less frequently and became agents of *Sovnarkom* (and therefore the Party leadership). Elections to the Soviets became less frequent and more subject to Party control and the All-Union Congress of Soviets and the Central Executive Committee *(Vtsik)* lost control over *Sovnarkom*. The Congress of Soviets had little power and met for only a few days each year. The Party apparatus, not the state apparatus, was where real power resided.

3. Centralisation of power within the Party leadership

During the Civil War, there was a growing trend for orders to be sent down from above and important posts, especially those of local Party secretaryships, were filled by appointment from above and not by election from below.

Until 1921 there was still considerable freedom of debate within the Party, for example, at the 9th Party Congress (1920), the Workers' Opposition, a faction within the Party, criticised the domination of the Party by the Central Committee and also the policy of War Communism.

However, because of the economic and political crises facing the Party in 1921, the 10th Party Congress passed the 'Resolution on Party Unity', which banned factions within the Party and made debate within the Party less open and public. The Workers' Opposition was banned and 150,000 members of the Party were purged.

4. Party membership expanded rapidly

The Civil War saw both a major expansion in Party membership and a growing bureaucratisation of the Party; growing numbers of Party members held administrative posts.

By 1921 there were 732,000 members; by 1933 Party membership had risen to over 3.5 million. Most of the new recruits were drawn from the working class whereas many of the old Bolsheviks had educated backgrounds. Historians tend to agree that this growth in the size and bureaucratisation of the Party facilitated Stalin's rise to power as he held the key positions within the Party administration.

2.4.1 The Stalin Constitution of 1936

In 1936, a new constitution, drafted by Bukharin, replaced the original constitution of the USSR. The main differences were that there were now more republics—eleven rather than the seven when the USSR was set up in 1923—and that the All-Union Congress was replaced by the Soviet of the Union and the Soviet of the Nationalities, which together made up the new Supreme Soviet. However, only candidates approved by the Communist Party could stand for election and the Supreme Soviet had no real power, meeting for just a few days each year.

The new 'Stalin Constitution' on paper granted Soviet citizens a range of democratic freedoms, including freedom of speech and liberty of conscience. However, this was just a façade, intended largely to impress foreign Socialists. The reality was The Great Terror: mass arrests, executions without trial and the proliferation of prison camps, administered by the *Gulag*.

 Key Term

Gulag: the agency that ran the prison camps in Stalin's USSR.

TOPICS:
The New Economic Policy

3.1 The New Economic Policy (1921–1928)

Facing economic collapse, famine, and widespread revolts, Lenin decided that War Communism had to be abandoned. In March 1921, at the Tenth Congress of the Communist Party, Lenin introduced his new economic policy (NEP). Many members of the Party were horrified by what they regarded as a retreat towards capitalism but Lenin demonstrated his leadership qualities by winning over the Congress.

Key Features of the NEP

- Private trade was restored to the countryside as grain requisitioning was ended. The peasants had to hand over 10% of their grain to the government, as a tax in kind, but were allowed to sell any surplus grain to private traders who became known as *Nepmen*.

- The old devalued rouble was replaced by a new more stable rouble.

- A mixture of socialism and capitalism prevailed in the urban economy. Larger factories and industrial concerns, such as steel plants and coal mines, the *'commanding heights of the economy'*, as Lenin called them, were to remain under state control. This meant that the state employed about 75% of the industrial workforce. NEP led to the reintroduction of private ownership of small and medium sized factories.

How successful was the NEP?

- NEP made possible a gradual recovery from the economic crisis of 1920–1921.
- By 1928, Russian industrial output had reached the 1914 level; agriculture recovered faster. In 1923 this led to what Trotsky dubbed the **'scissors crisis,'** where food prices were falling while the price of scarce manufactured goods remained high. Peasants could not afford the tools, pots and other manufactured goods that they needed.

TOPICS:
The Politburo
The struggle to succeed Lenin
Key historical perspectives

The struggle to succeed Lenin originated not with his death in 1924 but from 1922 when he suffered the first of a succession of strokes and was increasingly incapacitated. By 1929, Josef Stalin had emerged as the sole leader of the Communist Party but back in the early 1920s few Russians would have predicted his rise to power.

How was Stalin able to secure the leadership of the Communist Party?

1. Stalin was a member of the *Politburo* and *Orgburo*, the top committees within the Party and **he held several powerful positions within the Party apparatus**; in particular, Lenin appointed him General Secretary in 1922. He was able to use this to develop a power base within the Party, as he could promote and dismiss influential Party officials, particularly local Party secretaries. Stalin realised that the key to power lay in control over the Party organisation, rather than within state institutions. The Party grew rapidly, numbering 800,000 by 1925 and over 1.5 million by 1929. As its membership expanded, control over it became increasingly centralised, concentrating enormous power in Stalin's hands. Trotsky, Stalin's main rival for the leadership, although a hugely influential figure, and Commissar for War, held no significant position within the Party apparatus and so was unable to develop his own power base to compete with Stalin.

2. **Stalin's rivals underestimated him**. Lacking the charisma or the oratorical brilliance of Trotsky, the other leading figures in the Party ignored the 'grey blur', as Stalin was once dubbed, and concentrated their efforts on preventing Trotsky from gaining control over the Party.

3. Stalin was a very skilful political operator and was able to play off different factions within the Party leadership against each other.

These divisions were partly the result of:

- **Personal rivalries**, for example, Kamenev and Zinoviev resented Trotsky's arrogance and were prepared to work with Stalin against Trotsky in the period of 1922–1925. During this period, Stalin, Kamenev, and Zinoviev formed a three-man leadership team, known as the *'triumvirate'* or *'troika'*. They combined to force Trotsky's resignation as Commissar for War in 1925. Only in 1926 did Zinoviev and Kamenev decide to work with Trotsky in the so-called 'United Opposition', but by then it was too late to prevent Stalin removing them from the *Politburo*.

(continued)

Key Term

Collectivisation: the abolition of private ownership of land and its replacement by a system under which the peasants of a village or several villages owned the land jointly, though under the Communist Party's tight control.

How was Stalin able to secure the leadership of the Communist Party? *(continued)*

- **Major policy disagreements within the Party**. The Party was split over whether to continue with NEP or not. From 1923, those on the Left of the Party (e.g. Trotsky and Zinoviev) believed NEP should be replaced by rapid industrialisation and a move towards **collectivisation** of agriculture, whereas those on the Right (chiefly Bukharin) argued that NEP was working and should be maintained.

The other key policy dispute was over the issue of promoting worldwide revolution. The Left, particularly Trotsky, favoured 'Permanent Revolution', seeing international revolution as essential to the survival of socialism in Russia. By contrast, the Right adopted the slogan 'Socialism in One Country', arguing that, having witnessed the suppression of communist revolutions in Germany and Hungary, international revolution was not possible for the foreseeable future and so the Russian Communist Party must focus on establishing a socialist economy at home.

Stalin began by supporting the Right against the Left on the question of NEP and he used the support of the Right to remove the Left from the *Politburo* in 1926. Then from 1928, Stalin turned on the Right and attacked NEP, urging the Party to adopt rapid industrialisation and forced collectivisation. In 1929–1930, the Right (Bukharin, Rykov, and Tomsky) were removed from the *Politburo* and replaced by supporters of Stalin.

4. **Stalin was also much better than his rivals at gauging the mood of the ordinary Party members**. He realised that in the mid-1920s the Party had little interest in exporting revolution abroad, weary as it was after the upheavals of 1917–1921, and that most of the Party thought that NEP was a success in permitting economic recovery. Equally, Stalin judged correctly that most Communists had, by 1928–1929, begun to have serious reservations about NEP because economic growth was slowing down and the peasants were withholding grain from the markets in an attempt to force prices up. By the late 1920s, many in the Party were impatient to launch more socialist economic policies, such as collectivisation of agriculture, and wanted to transform the USSR into a modern industrial state.

5. **Stalin was able to outmanoeuvre Trotsky by appearing as the chief mourner at Lenin's funeral** (having misled Trotsky about its date) and then by promoting himself as the true heir of Lenin.

6. **Trotsky's health was poor** in 1924–1925, just when he needed to be at his strongest as the power struggle developed.

7. **Stalin was fortunate in that, following Lenin's death in January 1924, the Central Committee decided not to publish Lenin's** *Political Testament* in which Lenin had been deeply critical of Stalin (and somewhat less so of other leading Communists) and had recommended Stalin's dismissal as General Secretary.

8. **Stalin was able to use the Resolution on Party Unity (1921) to silence his opponents** within the top tiers of the Party by branding them as factions seeking to undermine Party unity. So, first Trotsky, Zinoviev and Kamenev were branded the 'Left Opposition' and later Bukharin, Tomsky and Rykov were labelled the 'Right Opposition'.

4.1 The *Politburo* (1924–1926)

'Left Communists'	'Right Communists'
Trotsky	Bukharin
Zinoviev	Tomsky
Kamenev	Rykov

Stalin moved his position between the Right and Left factions

4.2 The Struggle to Succeed Lenin

1922

- Stalin was appointed General Secretary of the Party
- Lenin suffered two strokes
- Triumvirate of Stalin, Zinoviev, and Kamenev formed collective leadership for the Party
- Lenin wrote his *Political Testament*

1923

- Lenin added a postscript to *Political Testament*, calling for Stalin's removal as General Secretary
- 'Scissors Crisis' led Trotsky and others on the Left to question NEP

1924

- Lenin's death
- Central Committee suppressed Lenin's *Political Testament*

1925

- Trotsky resigned as War Commissar
- Party Congress endorsed NEP and *Socialism in One Country*
- Zinoviev and Kamenev began to oppose Stalin

1926

- *United Opposition* of Trotsky, Zinoviev, and Kamenev
- *United Opposition* was removed from the *Politburo*
- Voroshilov and other allies of Stalin joined the *Politburo*

1927

- Zinoviev, Kamenev, and Trotsky were expelled from the Party
- Grain procurement crisis began as peasants withheld grain

1928

- Grain procurement crisis continued
- Stalin responded by requisitioning grain in the so-called *'Urals-Siberia method'*
- Bread rationing was introduced in Moscow and Leningrad
- First **Five Year Plan** was introduced; NEP was abandoned

1929 - 1930

- Party Congress set ambitious targets for the First Five Year Plan
- *Right Opposition* (Tomsky, Rykov, and Bukharin) was removed from the *Politburo*
- Trotsky was expelled from the USSR
- Collectivisation was introduced; the 'liquidation of the *kulaks*'

 Key Term

Five Year Plan: starting in 1928, Stalin introduced a series of economic plans under which the Soviet authorities set targets for every industry for a period of five years.

Figure 4.1: *Trotsky*

Figure 4.2: *Stalin*

4.3 Key Historical Perspectives: Stalin

Historians see Stalin's rise to power and the relationship between Stalinism and Leninism in a variety of different ways. Some argue that Stalin's rule represented a major deviation from that of Lenin, whilst others see a basic continuity in their methods. Some of the key interpretations are summarised below.

Key interpretations	
Structuralist approach (e.g. Richard Pipes)	• Regards Stalin as a product of Russia's circumstances: a strong ruler was required because the country was just emerging from nearly a decade of war and civil war. • Stalin was the natural successor to Lenin because of the way the Party had become increasingly bureaucratised.
Continuity between Leninism and Stalinism (e.g. Robert Conquest)	• Lenin created the single party dictatorship and system of terror, which Stalin continued. So, Stalin was the heir to the Leninist tradition.
Stalinism viewed as a deviation from Leninism (e.g. Stephen Cohen)	• Stalin distorted Lenin's legacy. Lenin used terror during the Civil War only as a temporary, emergency measure; Lenin allowed dissent within the Party; Lenin was hostile to a cult of the leader. Stalin, by contrast, used terror as a normal feature of government when the USSR was at peace; he suppressed debate within the Party; he created a personality cult of monstrous proportions. • Historians like Cohen argue that Communism could have developed in a very different, less brutal way if another leader, such as Bukharin, had succeeded Lenin.

TOPICS:
Collectivisation
Industrialisation
Key historical perspectives

Historians often use the phrase 'the Revolution from above' to characterise Stalin's economic policies in the 1930s. They argue that the economic changes brought about by Stalin and imposed on the Russian people represented much more of a transformation of society than the Bolsheviks' seizure of power in 1917. Stalin abandoned Lenin's New Economic Policy (NEP) and introduced rapid industrialisation in the guise of his Five Year Plans (1928 onwards) and forced collectivisation (from 1929).

Why did Stalin end NEP?

NEP had enabled the economy to recover, by 1926, from the effects of the First World War and Civil War, but economic growth slowed down thereafter.

- Lenin had presented NEP as a temporary retreat from socialism. By the late 1920s, many Communists were impatient to get on and build a modern, socialist economy; they wanted to pursue a more heroic vision than the tired compromise with capitalism that NEP represented.

- By 1927, several international developments seemed to threaten the USSR's security:

  ○ The coming to power in Poland of Marshal Pilsudski (1926), who was aggressively anti-communist

  ○ The breaking off of Russian-British diplomatic relations

  ○ The brutal massacre of Chinese communists by Chiang Kai-shek's Nationalists in 1927.

This 'war scare' appeared to highlight the need for Russia to catch up in industrial terms with the West and, for that to happen, Stalin argued that the modernisation of agriculture, by means of collectivisation, was also essential.

As Stalin later put it in a speech in 1931:

We are fifty or a hundred years behind the advanced countries. We must make good this distance in ten years. Either we do it, or we shall be crushed. This is what our obligations to the workers and peasants of the USSR dictate to us.

(continued)

Why did Stalin end NEP? *(continued)*

- There were serious food shortages in 1927–1928 because the peasants and the state were at loggerheads. The government had cut the price they paid for the peasants' grain in order to find the resources to invest in industrial expansion. The peasants retaliated by marketing less of the grain that they grew.

- Stalin responded to this 'grain procurement crisis' by reviving forced grain requisitioning when he visited Siberia in 1927. Stalin judged his 'Urals-Siberia method' a success and this seems to have prompted him to turn to collectivisation as a means of achieving greater state control over the grain supply.

- Stalin and many others in the Party saw collectivisation as a means of eliminating class enemies, the *'kulaks'* or rich, 'exploiting' peasants, who could be presented as 'petty capitalists'. Collectivisation was consistent with Marxist-Leninist principles: collective ownership would replace private ownership. All factions within the Communist Party had agreed that the peasantry should be encouraged to join collective farms but Right Communists like Bukharin argued against forced collectivisation. However, on the eve of collectivisation less than 3% of Russia's agricultural land was collectivised, suggesting that voluntary collectivisation would not be successful.

- Stalin viewed forced collectivisation as the way to provide the surplus manpower, food, and money required for rapid industrialisation. Stalin and his supporters believed that larger farm units—the collectives—would be more efficient than the old small peasant farms. Current Russian grain yields were only half of those in Germany. Stalin assumed that more grain would be grown, which could be used to feed an enlarged industrial workforce and for export abroad to earn the foreign currency to buy foreign machinery needed to equip Russia's factories.

- Stalin's motivation for collectivisation was also political. The peasants had never been enthusiastic supporters of the Communist Party and the Party had only achieved limited control over the countryside. The new collectives were to be run by a Party-appointed chairman and the new Motor Tractor Stations each had an **NKVD** (secret police) unit attached to them. Thus, the peasants would be brought much more firmly under the Party's control.

Key Term

NKVD: initials by which the state security police was known in the 1930s; under Lenin it had been known as the *Cheka*.

Key Term

Dekulakisation: term for the campaign against those peasants, known as *'kulaks'*, who were allegedly better off; under this process, many peasants were dispossessed of their land, killed or sent to prison camps.

5.1 Collectivisation

Stalin's policy of collectivisation constituted a revolution in the countryside, forcing 25 million peasant households into 240,000 collective farms. In the process, the peasants' traditional way of life based on the village commune and attachment to the Orthodox Church was destroyed. Millions died in the process and millions more fled from the villages into the growing industrial cities. Collectivisation and rapid industrialisation were inextricably linked.

'Dekulakisation'

The forced collectivisation programme of 1929–1930 was in effect a declaration of war against the peasants by the Party. Stalin launched collectivisation by attacking the *kulaks* or richer peasants. In practice the term *'kulak'* was applied to any peasant who resisted forced collectivisation. In December 1929, Stalin announced that the Party aimed at 'liquidating the *kulak* as a class'. The Party recruited 25,000 urban activists and sent them, supported by the Red Army and NKVD, into the countryside to implement collectivisation.

> **Why did Stalin start by attacking the** *kulaks?*
> - Because the *kulaks* were viewed as petty **bourgeoisie** since they owned and often rented out land. Their elimination was therefore a further step towards the creation of a 'classless' society.
> - 'Dekulakisation' served as a warning to the peasantry of the consequences of not co-operating with the Party.

 Key Term

Bourgeoisie: in Marxist terms, those who own the means of producing wealth and who exploit the 'proletariat', who did not own the means of production.

In the winter of 1929–1930, in the region of 1.5 million '*kulaks*' were dispossessed of their land. Many were forcibly deported to Siberia or Central Asia or were killed while many others fled to the towns. There was widespread peasant resistance to collectivisation and not just by the richer peasants. Party activists responded savagely but peasants continued to defy them by slaughtering their livestock rather than handing it over to the collectives.

5.2 Key Historical Perspectives: Why Did Stalin Call a Temporary Halt to Collectivisation in 1930?

> **Why did Stalin call a temporary halt to Collectivisation in 1930?**
>
> By the beginning of 1930, 55% of farmland had been collectivised but in March Stalin announced that collectivisation had to be voluntary and, an article in *Pravda* (the Party newspaper) entitled 'Dizzy with Success', accused Party officials of excessive force.
>
> Most historians have interpreted this as a cynical ploy by Stalin to encourage the peasants to co-operate so that the success of the 1930 harvest would not be compromised by the upheavals.
>
> Other historians, such as Lynne Viola, argue that collectivisation did get out of control and that Stalin was genuinely trying to reassert central government's control over local officials and activists in order to end the chaotic conditions prevailing in the countryside.

Forced collectivisation reinstated (1931)

From the beginning of 1931 the Party reverted to forced requisitioning. This time it was accompanied by limited concessions to the peasants: they were permitted to retain small private plots of land (averaging 0.3 hectare) and some livestock. By 1935, over 90% of farmland had been collectivised. The Party set up a small number of state farms (*Sovkhoz*) in which the peasants worked for a wage but the majority of peasants were organised into collectives *(Kolkhoz)*. There were on average seventy-six families in each collective and the peasants had to deliver to the state a fixed quota of produce at prices set by the state. The peasants were allowed to retain any surplus grain (after the state quota was delivered) but they also had to pay the Motor Tractor Stations, set up in the 1930s, from which they rented tractors. However, tractors were in short supply in the early 1930s.

The famine (1932–1933)

In this period millions of peasants died in a man-made famine. Estimates range from 4 to 6.5 million deaths. The disruption caused by collectivisation, and by peasant resistance to it, resulted in falling grain output but what transformed that into a famine was the fact that the state took a far higher percentage of the harvest, leaving the peasants to starve. Non-Russian areas, particularly the Ukraine, suffered most. In Kazakhstan, the population fell by 20% in the 1930s.

Did Stalin achieve his aims in collectivising agriculture?

YES

- ✓ The Party now had much greater control over the peasants and the countryside. Collectivisation has often been termed by historians as a new form of 'serfdom' for the peasants.

- ✓ More importantly for Stalin, the state now had much greater control over the grain supply. Whereas in 1928 the state procured (obtained) 15% of the harvest; by 1935, this had risen to 35%. In 1933, grain procurements had peaked at 40%.

- ✓ The increased grain procurements enabled the state to feed an expanded industrial workforce, although this was only true after 1935 because the chaos of the early stages of collectivisation resulted in food rationing for the towns. Higher grain procurements also meant more could be exported abroad in order to purchase machinery to equip Russia's new factories. Russia exported 5 million tons of grain a year in 1931–1932 and even during the terrible famine 2 million tons of grain a year were sold abroad.

- ✓ Collectivisation led to a massive increase in the urban population, which grew by 12 million in the first five years of collectivisation. This provided the workforce for Russia's developing industries under the Five Year Plans.

NO

- ✗ Grain production and overall agricultural productivity increased only marginally:
  - In 1913 Russia's population produced 0.5 tons of grain per head
  - By 1937, this had increased fractionally to 0.57 tons per head.

  Collectivisation did not lead to greater efficiency because the peasants lacked the incentives to work hard on the land belonging to the collectives.

- ✗ The collectives remained inefficient in the long-term too. By the 1960s, the USSR was obliged to purchase large amounts of grain from Canada and the USA. By contrast, the peasants did work hard on their small private plots, which, though only constituting 5% of the USSR's arable land, produced 25% of its fruit and vegetables.

- ✗ Livestock levels in the USSR fell massively and did not fully recover until the 1950s. By the early 1930s, the peasants had slaughtered 65% of their sheep and 46% of their cattle.

5.3 Rapid Industrialisation (1928–1941)

The First Five Year Plan (1928–1932)

Three years after the First Five Year Plan (FFYP from here on) was launched, Stalin made it clear in a speech he made in 1931 (referred to on page 39) that the tempo of industrialisation could not be lessened because Russia was behind its capitalist enemies. The USSR was the world's sole socialist state, with the exception of Outer Mongolia, and Stalin therefore saw rapid industrialisation as essential to safeguard Russia from attack. His motivation was similar to that of Tsar Alexander III and Tsar Nicholas II when they initiated industrialisation programmes in the 1890s in an attempt to revive Russia's status as a great power.

At the 15th Party Congress in December 1927, several possible sets of targets for industrial expansion were debated. The Central State Planning Commission in Moscow, known as Gosplan, drew up a range of possible targets for industrial expansion. Towards the end of 1928, the Central Committee adopted the most ambitious of the targets but it was not until the 16th Party Congress, held in April 1929, that the targets for the FFYP were officially fixed. The FFYP ended private ownership in industry, thereby abandoning Lenin's New Economic Policy. The FFYP aimed at a massive 236% increase in total industrial output. The 'command economy' was born, with targets set by Gosplan for factories all over the USSR.

Stalin saw the whole enterprise in heroic and military terms and used military language in exhorting the population to smash targets and create a modern socialist economy in the process. Stalin declared that:

> There are no fortresses that Bolsheviks cannot storm.

The FFYP was chaotically managed, with targets being constantly revised upwards and Stalin deciding to complete the plan in four years. Centralised planning led to many mistakes being made, as did the fact that 9 million of the workers recently recruited into the new factories were unskilled peasants. 1,500 new factories were constructed by the end of 1932, many of them in previously undeveloped areas east of the Ural Mountains, for example, Magnitogorsk was built from scratch as a vast steel-producing centre. The prestigious Moscow Metro (underground) project was begun along with the Volga-White Sea Canal.

The Second Five Year Plan (1933–1937)

To some extent in drawing up the Second Five Year Plan, the Communist leadership learnt from its mistakes in the FFYP and set lower targets for industrial expansion. The period 1934–1935 saw great success as many of the factories built under the FFYP were now up and running. Food rationing was ended in 1935. However, from 1936 the Second Plan was disrupted by the *Stakhanovite* movement, which sought to encourage the workers to emulate the record-breaking exploits of the coal-miner, Alexi Stakhanov, and led to 'storming' methods where factories worked around the clock to maximise production. However, this approach led to machinery being broken and industrial workers becoming exhausted. Stalin's **Purges**, from 1936 onwards, led to hundreds of thousands of skilled workers, engineers, and managers being sent to the labour camps or executed.

The Third Five-Year Plan (1938–1941)

The main focus was on industries linked to rearmament because Stalin became increasingly fearful of an attack by Hitler's Germany. The Third Five Year Plan was cut short by the Nazi invasion of June 1941.

'Carrot and Stick' Methods

Stalin used a range of methods to try to achieve his goal of transforming the USSR into an industrial superpower.

'Carrot'

- Higher wages were introduced for skilled workers and for exceeding targets (1931). Both practices ran counter to Marxist principles.

- Propaganda. The *Stakhanovite* movement encouraged workers to smash targets and those who did were rewarded with medals and dubbed 'heroes of socialist labour', feted in the Soviet press. Also, Socialist Realist art celebrated the achievements of the Five Year Plans.

- *Komsomol* (the Young Communist League) activists voluntarily contributed to some key projects, such as building Magnitogorsk.

Key Term

Purges: the large-scale removal and punishment of Communist Party members, officials and managers. To 'purge' is to cleanse by removing a harmful or unwanted element from something.

'Stick'

⊗ **'Iron discipline'** in the factories. Workers were threatened by harsh punishments for absenteeism or for not meeting quotas.

⊗ 1932 saw the reintroduction of internal passports which had been abolished in 1917. This made it difficult for workers to switch jobs or move from town to town, as any move had to be approved by the Party, with a worker's passport stamped to show this.

⊗ Prison camp labour was widely used, e.g. 70,000 prisoners died constructing the Belomor Canal.

⊗ There were a number of 'Show Trials' of managers and engineers, who were accused of 'wrecking' and industrial sabotage on behalf of capitalist powers, which were designed to terrorise the workforce into compliance with the state's demands on them and to provide a justification for any shortcomings of the Five Year Plans. The first such trial was the Shakhty Trial (1928) of fifty-three engineers, five of whom were executed.

How did Stalin find the resources to industrialise?

- By taking more grain from the peasants and then using it to feed the growing towns and to export it in order to buy foreign machinery
- By heavy taxation
- By driving down living standards; the historian Leonard Schapiro has calculated that Russian living standards by 1940 were half of those in 1928
- By massively increasing the industrial workforce (Russia's urban population almost doubled to 56 million in the 1930s), recruiting peasants who were fleeing collectivisation and also greater numbers of women factory workers.

How successful were Stalin's Five Year Plans?

- Official Soviet statistics, produced during and after Stalin's rule, about the increases in industrial production achieved during the 1930s are very suspect not just because they were inflated for propaganda purposes, but also because of the falsification of figures by managers desperate to avoid punishment for non-fulfilment of targets. Nonetheless, Western historians agree that the 1930s saw a huge expansion of Soviet industry.

	1927	1939
Coal (millions of tons)	35	125
Pig iron (millions of tons)	12	40

Some figures relating to industrial output in Russia: 1927-39; Source: David Warnes, 'Russia: A Modern History'

The 'upside' of the Five Year Plans

⊕ The USSR's **Gross Domestic Product** (GDP) tripled during 1928–1940, whereas no other major economy came close to even doubling output. For much of the 1930s the major capitalist countries were still in the throes of the Great Depression.

⊕ The USSR in 1928 had been behind the USA, Britain, Germany and France in terms of industrial output and only just ahead of Japan; by 1940 Soviet output was bettered only by the USA. Arguably without this expansion the USSR's victory over Nazi Germany in 1941–1945 would not have been possible.

(↑) Comparing production figures for 1927–1928 and 1940, western historians estimate a fourfold increase in coal and electricity production between 1927 and 1940, and a sixfold increase in steel. Oil production 'only' doubled in this period, but this was one area of industry where Russia was already a world leader in 1927.

(↑) Huge projects like the Dnieper Dam and the Moscow Metro were completed. 8,000 new factories and industrial enterprises were built.

(↑) The USSR was transformed into an industrial society in terms of the increase in urban population, from 26 million (1926) to 56 million by 1939.

(↑) The literacy rate increased from 51% to 81% of the population, as the Party recognised the need for a more educated workforce. 70,000 libraries were built. Technical colleges turned out 300,000 engineering graduates in the 1930s.

The 'downside' of the Five-Year Plans

(↓) Although Gosplan's centralised planning proved successful in expanding the volume of industrial output, it was far from successful in ensuring quality. The USSR still lagged behind the West in this respect. This is illustrated by the huge difference in the durability of Soviet goods and the duplication of certain machine parts and a lack of others.

(↓) John Scott, in his book *Behind the Urals*, provides an explanation for why many Soviet projects ran into difficulties and why much of what was produced was poor quality; many of the industrial workers were recently recruited peasants, who "were completely unfamiliar with industrial tools and processes."

(↓) The FYPs suffered from the effects of what some historians term 'gigantomania': Stalin was obsessed with huge projects. Some of them were totally misconceived, e.g. the Belomor Canal, which was too shallow to take the warships for which it was designed.

(↓) Although the USSR had risen to the rank of the world's second industrial power by 1940, this expansion had been very largely focused on heavy industry. Consumer goods production rose during the 1930s but by only a third of the increase in iron output as this was a low priority for Stalin. In this respect the USSR did not catch up with the West.

In the long-term, the 'Command Economy' did not work; after the Second World War, Soviet industry stagnated and the technological gap (except in certain defence industries) with the West widened. Western historians generally argue that the collapse of Soviet Communism at the end of the 1980s owed much to the inefficiency and lack of incentives that characterised both collectivised agriculture and the state-owned and directed industrial sector.

5.4 Key Historical Perspectives: Could the USSR Have Closed the Gap Economically with the West Without Stalin's Methods?

Could the USSR have closed the gap economically with the West without Stalin's methods?

Answer: 'No'

Historians such as Alec Nove argue that, without Stalin's brutal methods and unslackening pace, Russia would not have caught up with the West and would not have been able to survive Hitler's invasion in 1941. They argue that Stalin made a unique contribution to industrialisation in accelerating the whole process, abandoning the cautious approach of Bukharin and other leading Communists, and by finding the resources to transform Russia without the foreign investment that had characterised rapid industrialisation under the last two Tsars. Left Communists like Trotsky and Preobrazhensky had, in the 1920s, attacked NEP because they believed it would not permit large-scale industrial expansion.

Answer: 'Yes'

Other historians such as Robert Conquest claim that similar industrial growth rates to those of the 1930s could have been achieved by continuing NEP. They point out that Stalin's methods were often counter-productive, for example over-centralised planning stifled local initiative and 'storming' caused accidents and often led to a fall in productivity as workers became exhausted. As importantly, they rightly emphasise the fact that Stalin's other policies undermined the FYPs. The purges of 1936–1938 destroyed many talented managers and engineers; collectivisation led to food shortages in the towns until 1935.

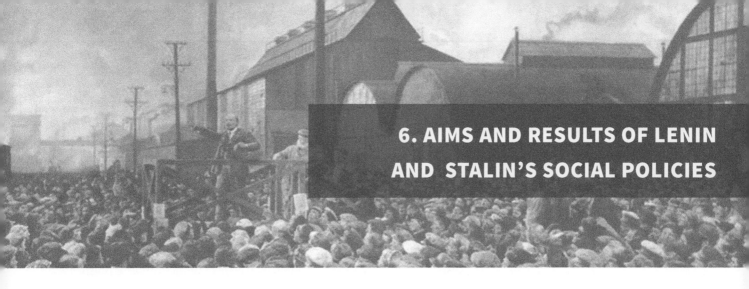

TOPICS:
Religion
National minorities
Education
Women and the family

6.1 Communist Party Policy Towards Religion

Karl Marx was an atheist who famously wrote that:

Religion is the opium of the people.

meaning that the ruling classes used religion to ensure obedience from the exploited working classes.

6.1.1 The Orthodox Church

In October 1917, the Bolsheviks confiscated all of the Church's lands. During the Russian Civil War (1918-1920), the Bolsheviks killed many Orthodox Christian Priests because the Orthodox clergy tended to support the Whites. Most Orthodox Bishops were arrested in the 1920s.

The Communist Party sought to eradicate religious belief by:

- Organising anti-religious propaganda; in 1926, the Party created the League of Militant Atheists to carry out this function.

- A decree of 1929 barred churches from participating in any activities other than church services.

- Persecution of Orthodox Christians increased after 1929 as part of Stalin's attack on the peasants' traditional way of life during collectivisation. OGPU (secret police) agents, volunteers from the League of Militant Atheists, and other Communist Party activists were employed to attack churches, destroying church bells and religious art. Many churches were transformed into storehouses, cinemas, or meeting halls. By the end of the 1930s, only 2% of churches were still operating. Stalin did allow a small number of churches to remain open, so that he could claim that the freedom of worship promised in the 1936 Stalin Constitution was being observed.

- Many Priests and churchgoers were arrested or executed during Stalin's '**Great Terror**'. Of 163 Orthodox Bishops active in 1930, just twelve were still so by 1939.

However, the persecution outlined above does not mean that the party had eliminated religious belief; in the 1937 Census, 57% of Russians said that they were believers.

> **Key Term**
>
> **The 'Great Terror':**
> term used to describe the high point of Stalin's purges when hundreds of thousands of people were arrested and/or executed in the mid to late 1930s.

Probably as a consequence of this, the leaders of the League of Militant Atheists were purged. Persecution of the Orthodox Church was lessened during the **Great Patriotic War** of 1941-1945 as Stalin sought to use The Church to rally support for the defence of his regime by appealing to a more traditional Russian patriotism.

6.1.2 Muslims

In the 1920s, the Soviet state had persecuted Muslims less than the Orthodox Church. However, in the 1930s this changed dramatically and 95% of mosques were closed down.

6.2 Communist Party Policy Towards National Minorities

In 1917, non-Russians had made up around half of Russia's population. The Bolsheviks had denounced the Tsarist Empire as the 'prison-house of the peoples' and, in the Decree on Nationalities (1917), Lenin had promised that the various nationalities of the former Tsarist empire would be allowed to choose to be independent. The Bolsheviks had assumed that socialist revolution, industrialisation, and urbanisation would, over time, erode separate national consciousness and ethnic differences.

6.2.1 Policy in the 1920s

Once Bolshevik victory in the Civil War was certain, Lenin went back on his promises to the non-Russian peoples; as the Red Army captured non-Russian areas during the Civil War, they imposed Communist rule on them and turned them into Soviet Socialist Republics, which were formally incorporated into the Union of Soviet Socialist Republics (USSR) under a new constitution introduced in 1923. The USSR was a multi-national federal system, with a range of powers granted to the republics at local level and others reserved to the Soviet authorities at the centre in Moscow.

Initially, Communist Party policy towards the non-Russian nationalities rejected the 'Russification' approach taken by Tsars Alexander III and Nicholas II (1881-1917). Instead, the Bolsheviks promoted '*korenizatsiia*'–that is, 'indigenisation'–whereby non-Russian languages and cultural expressions were tolerated in an attempt to reconcile the non-Russians to the new Soviet state. The Bolsheviks believed that this permissive approach would result in a '*flowering of national cultures that are socialist in content and national in form*'.[1]

During the period of NEP, the Soviet authorities took a conciliatory approach to their dealings with Muslim areas, and across the USSR encouraged education in the local vernacular language. Ukrainian had been banned from local schools before 1917 but by 1927, over 90% of Ukrainian children were studying it at school. Local languages were also used in administration. Moreover, the Communist Party appointed increasing numbers of officials drawn from ethnic minorities to party and state posts in each republic.

6.2.2 Policy under Stalin

The measures discussed above had unintended consequences; non-Russian national consciousness had been stimulated by the policy of 'indigenisation' and ethnic minority officials put local interests before those of Moscow and the USSR as a whole.

Therefore, in 1933 Stalin announced that anti-Soviet, bourgeois elements were promoting nationalism in an attempt to undermine the Soviet system and undermine the socialist revolution. This effectively meant the end to 'indigenisation' and a return to the policy of Russification pursued by Tsars Alexander III and Nicholas II under which the government tried to impose the Russian language and Orthodox Christian faith on the non-Russians. This abrupt change of official policy towards the non-Russian nationalities is explained

---

[1] Stalin, J. V., (1952) *Works,* Moscow: Foreign Languages Publishing House

by Stalin's collectivisation drive which, since 1928, had increased tensions between the Soviet authorities and non-Russian minorities because the process involved a massive centralisation drive as the power of the Party was directed towards a radical assault on the peasants' traditional way of life and on the Orthodox Church.

Resistance to collectivisation was greatest among the non-Russian nationalities, particularly in the Ukraine (whose 40 million people made it the second largest republic within the USSR) and Kazakhstan. Repression of Ukrainian peasants who resisted collectivisation, involving mass executions, arrests, and deportations, was accompanied by a campaign against Ukrainian nationalism. Ethnic Ukrainian officials were largely replaced by Russians. From 1933 onwards, there was an increasing emphasis placed on promoting the Russian language, culture and history throughout the USSR. Nonetheless, despite this new approach, non-Russian novelists were still encouraged to write in their native languages, as long as they conformed to 'Socialist Realism' and rejected 'bourgeois-nationalist' themes that might undermine the Soviet system.

During Stalin's purges, there was increased repression of the non-Russian minorities; in 1937–1938, over 30% of executions carried out were in connection with ethnic minority issues.

6.3 Communist Party Policy Towards Education

6.3.1 Policy in the 1920s

The Party made tackling illiteracy a major priority right from the start. Only 40% of adult males were literate in 1913; by 1926 this had risen to 70%, and by 1939 to 94%.

The People's Commissariat for Enlightenment, led by Anatoly Lunarcharsky, sought to increase educational opportunities for the working classes. In the 1920s progressive educational reforms were introduced in the USSR; examinations and uniforms were abolished. From 1928, it became increasingly difficult for anyone with a bourgeois background to gain access to higher education as the regime sought to train up a new generation of 'Red specialists' to replace its dependence on 'bourgeois specialists.' Komsomol and trade unions nominated around 150,000 bright young workers to undergo training at higher education institutions; they made up one third of the total student population in the period 1929-1932. Many of them were then recruited into the party and state administrative apparatuses. Most of the universities and polytechnics were broken up and reorganised to cater for more vocational courses.

6.3.2 Policy Under Stalin

Although during the 1930s the state, responding to the needs of the Five Year Plans, continued to expand technical and vocational training at the expense of more academic courses, Stalin did reverse some of the more progressive elements of earlier Soviet educational policy. In the 1930s, uniforms (including compulsory pigtails for girls) and exams were reintroduced into schools. A more traditional curriculum had reappeared by 1935 and, from December 1935, it was no longer a requirement to be of working class background to be admitted to higher education.

The Party placed a great emphasis on expanding educational provision during the 1930s, in order to provide the educated workforce required in the newly industrialised USSR. In 1930, all children were obliged to have a minimum of four years of primary education. By 1939, it was compulsory for children to have seven years of schooling. However, in 1940, school fees of between 300 and 400 roubles a year were introduced for the last three years of secondary schooling, meaning that children of Communist Party officials had the advantage in gaining access to higher education.

6.3.3 Youth Movements

The Communist Party sought to mobilise young people and mould their developing minds so that they became committed Communists. Young people aged 14-28 were recruited into Komsomol (the Young Communist League); between the ages of 9 and 14, children joined the All-Union Lenin Pioneer Organisation; younger children belonged to the Little Octobrists.

6.4 Communist Party Policy Towards Women and the Family

6.4.1 Policy under Lenin

Following the Bolshevik Revolution, divorce was made much easier and abortion was legalised. The impact of this legislation and the huge upheavals accompanying the introduction of the Five Year Plans, which occasioned huge social mobility, resulted in extremely high divorce rates; by 1937, 37% of all marriages in Moscow ended in divorce. Abortion rates also soared, with 154,000 abortions carried out in Moscow in 1934 compared to there being just 57,000 live births.

6.4.2 Policy under Stalin

By contrast, Stalin adopted a more traditional approach to family life, partly because he wanted to increase Russia's population in the belief that this would strengthen the USSR:

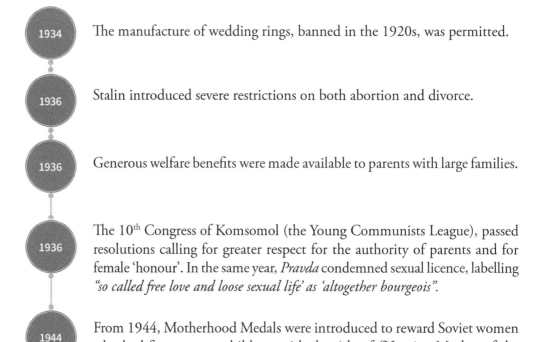

1934 The manufacture of wedding rings, banned in the 1920s, was permitted.

1936 Stalin introduced severe restrictions on both abortion and divorce.

1936 Generous welfare benefits were made available to parents with large families.

1936 The 10th Congress of Komsomol (the Young Communists League), passed resolutions calling for greater respect for the authority of parents and for female 'honour'. In the same year, *Pravda* condemned sexual licence, labelling *"so called free love and loose sexual life' as 'altogether bourgeois".*

1944 From 1944, Motherhood Medals were introduced to reward Soviet women who had five or more children, with the title of "Heroine Mother of the Soviet Union" reserved for women giving birth to ten or more children.

In the 1930s, in other ways, Stalin could be seen to have undermined traditional family life by encouraging women to work in factories, for example by providing crèche and canteen facilities. By 1940, there were 2 million nursery places available for babies and infants up to the age of seven. The Five-Year Plans saw a huge expansion in the numbers of women factory workers, increasing from 3 million (1928) to 13 million (1940). Many of the heroes of the *Stakhanovite* movement in both industry and agriculture were women, such as one Moscow farm labourer who reputedly broke the world record for harvesting cabbages! Although most women worked in low skilled sectors such as textiles and agriculture, by 1939 one third of Soviet engineers were women and 79% of doctors were women.

TOPICS:
Terror and purges
Propaganda
The cult of personality
Foreign policy

7.1 The Role of Force

7.1.1 The Great Terror (1936–1938)

'Terror' and 'Purges' were regular features of the USSR in the 1920s and 1930s. Even in the relatively calm years of NEP (1921–1928), 450,000 people had been arrested for 'counter-revolutionary activities'. Lenin had set up a secret police and prison camp system as a means of eliminating class enemies and suppressing political opposition. He had purged the Communist Party of 150,000 members in 1921, which meant they were expelled from the Party. This was in order to eliminate those who were not committed to the Party but had joined simply to further their careers; Trotsky termed them 'radishes'—red on the outside but white inside.

In a sense the Great Terror of 1936–1938 was simply a continuation of the dictatorial methods employed by Lenin. The continuity between Lenin's policies and those of Stalin seemed to be confirmed by a mass reform campaign in 1933–1934 when a Party Control Commission expelled 20% of the Party membership. However, what Stalin did next was quantitatively and qualitatively different from anything seen before in the USSR. Stalin purged over one third of the entire Party membership and executed about 600,000 of them. This was accompanied by sweeping purges of the armed forces and the imprisonment of millions of ordinary Soviet citizens. The prison camps mushroomed all over the country, under the control of the *Gulag*, which administered the camp system.

Prominent old Bolsheviks and senior military commanders were convicted at much publicised **Show Trials** but the fates of the mass of ordinary victims went unreported. It wasn't until Mikhail Gorbachev came into power in the late 1980s that the Party openly revealed and discussed the Terror of the 1930s. Foreign historians have only gained access to Soviet archives since the collapse of Communism but that access has already led historians to revise their thinking on the scale and causes of the Great Terror.

 Key Term

Show Trials: term used for the public trials held in the USSR in the mid to late 1930s under which leading members of the Communist Party and the Red Army were tried for treason against the party. The word 'show' is used because the trials were widely regarded as rigged, with the guilt of the accused already decided by the authorities.

A Timeline of Terror

1928 — The Shakty Trial: fifty-five engineers in the Donbass region charged with sabotaging industrial production.

1930 — The Trial of the 'Industrial Party': show trial of leading figures in the state industrial research and planning institutions, including Gosplan.

1932 — Riutin, former Moscow Party Secretary, circulated a document attacking Stalin as *"the evil genius of the Revolution"*. Riutin was expelled from the Party after Stalin had unsuccessfully demanded his execution.

1933 -1934 — 20% of Communist Party members were expelled.

1934 — At the Seventeenth Party Congress, Sergei Kirov gained more votes than Stalin in the elections to the Party's Central Committee. It later transpired that Stalin had many of the voting papers cast for Kirov destroyed, so that, although Kirov was still re-elected to the Central Committee, it appeared that more members had voted for Stalin.

1934 — The murder of Kirov, Secretary of the Leningrad Party (December). Historians are divided over whether Stalin was responsible. Robert Conquest argues Stalin was; while Isaac Deutscher believes Stalin was not behind the murder but decided to use it to justify the purges that followed. Stalin immediately issued a decree giving increased powers to the NKVD (secret police) in dealing with terrorist suspects. Thousands of Party members in Leningrad were arrested, accused of involvement in Kirov's murder.

1936 — The 'Trial of the 16': Kamenev, Zinoviev, and fourteen other 'Old Bolsheviks' were put on show trial, convicted and executed for alleged involvement in Kirov's murder and in a 'Trotskyite' conspiracy. Yagoda, the NKVD chief, was arrested and replaced by Yezhov.

1937 — The 'Trial of the 17': the 'Anti-Soviet Trotskyist Centre' were tried for plotting with Germany. Those executed included Radek. Torture was officially legalised. The Decree on 'Anti-Soviet Elements' led to regional arrest quotas for the NKVD, which was instructed to execute 28% of those arrested. Official Soviet figures record 353,000 executions in 1937 but this is probably an under-reporting.

1937 — Marshal Tukhachevsky, Soviet commander-in-chief, and seven other generals were convicted and executed after show trials. Over 35,000 army officers were arrested in the period 1937–1938.

1938 — The 'Trial of the 21': the 'Trotskyite-Rightists' were put on show trial. The most prominent victims were Bukharin and Rykov. NKVD records report 328,000 people executed (again probably an under-estimate).

1939   The Terror was scaled down. Yezhov had been arrested in 1938 and was replaced by Beria. The NKVD itself was now purged; the Soviet historian Dimitri Volkogonov estimates that 23,000 NKVD agents were executed.

1940   Trotsky was assassinated in Mexico by a Stalinist agent.

Why did the Great Terror happen?

- To an extent Stalin's purges were, like those of Lenin, motivated by a desire to keep the Party disciplined and loyal, particularly as it had grown so enormously by 1933. However, Stalin's Purges were on a totally different scale both in terms of the number of victims and the savagery of the process. Stalin's Terror was driven by certain motives which did not underlie Lenin's repression.

- Stalin was intent on building up and retaining his own personal power. He used the purges to remove 'Old Bolshevik' rivals like Zinoniev and Kamenev. Stalin had defeated these Old Bolsheviks in the 1920s but they still had some influence within the Party; for example, Rykov, Tomsky and Bukharin had been reinstated on to the Party's Central Committee in 1929. Stalin used the Show Trials to not just eliminate his former rivals but also to destroy their reputation, so that he alone could take the credit for the Communist Party's achievements. Yezhov, the NKVD chief, was a powerful force behind the purges and the NKVD undoubtedly saw the purges as an opportunity to increase their own power and influence within the USSR.

- Stalin's personality undoubtedly played a key part: he was vain, mistrustful, and unforgiving and took a pleasure in humiliating rivals and opponents. The historian **Robert Conquest** in particular has presented Stalin as the architect and driving force behind the Terror. There is plenty of evidence of Stalin's personal involvement in the Terror, for example, his signature on many lists of those to be arrested and executed.

- Stalin seems to have had genuine cause for concern about opposition to his economic policies within the Party. Certainly Riutin and, to a lesser extent, Kirov had voiced serious doubts about forced collectivisation. It seems very likely that Stalin was responsible for Kirov's murder in 1934, which he then used as an excuse to embark on a series of purges on an unprecedented scale.

7.1.2 Key Historical Perspectives: Stalin's Purges

The Totalitarian Perspective

According to the Totalitarian school of historians, Stalin's purges were a natural progression from the highly centralised, repressive system created by Lenin; the purges grew out of 'the logic of Bolshevism'. Stalin, according to Robert Conquest in the slogan of the 1930s, was 'the Lenin of today', but a more brutal and suspicious leader.

The Revisionist Perspective

Revisionist historians such as J. Arch Getty and Sheila Fitzpatrick argue that it is wrong simply to blame Stalin's paranoia for the purges. Though he did see enemies everywhere, at the same time other members of the Party either supported the purges because they could thereby eliminate their rivals and win promotion or because they believed it was a necessary part of the battle to build socialism.

(continued)

The Revisionist Perspective *(continued)*

Revisionist historians have challenged the traditional view of an all-powerful Stalin and an all-powerful Communist Party; they argue that the central leadership's control over the localities was never complete and that key policies such as dekulakisation and the purges generated a dynamic of their own, with the leadership in Moscow losing control to some extent of the processes they had unleashed.

The context for the purges must be considered; they followed the violent campaign to enforce collectivisation and the USSR appeared threatened by the rise of Nazi Germany and Japanese expansionism.

What were the effects of the Great Terror?

- 600,000 Party members lost their lives in the 1930s.
- Starting with the Commander-in-Chief, Tukhachevsky, Stalin removed almost half of the Red Army senior officers. This greatly weakened the Red Army, as shown in the Finnish War in 1939–1940 and encouraged Hitler's invasion, with nearly fatal consequences.
- Millions of ordinary, innocent Russians ended up in the Gulag. They endured terrible conditions, particularly in the freezing conditions of the Siberian camps. At least 70,000 prisoners died constructing the Belomor Canal. Historians have argued over the number of victims of the Terror. Robert Conquest estimates that between 7 and 8 million people were sent to the camps, of whom about 2 million died. Dimitri Volkogonov has suggested the much higher figures of 16 million prison camp inmates and 7 million deaths.
- A climate of fear gripped the Soviet people as no one knew who might or might not be an informer. Stalin intended thereby to terrorise the population into obedience.
- The purges' disruptive effects were felt in industry where the arrest of large numbers of engineers and managers seriously undermined the Second Five Year Plan and accounts for Stalin's reduction in the scale of the purges in 1939. Nonetheless the purges had the permanent effect of stifling initiative.
- Stalin's domination over the Party was now complete. To a large extent, Stalin had created a new party, by means of the purges, who owed unswerving loyalty to him. Stalin did not call a single Party Congress, which was supposed to meet every three years, between 1939 and 1952.
- The cult of Stalin, underway since his 50th birthday celebrations in 1929, expanded hugely. Stalin supplanted Lenin as the most important symbol of the Party. Stalin's image was ubiquitous, appearing on posters or in the form of statues and paintings. In a way, Stalin's icon took the place of the religious imagery swept away by the Bolshevik Revolution. The personality cult encouraged ordinary Russians to regard Stalin as a father figure, the genius who guided every aspect of national life.

7.2 The Role of Propaganda and the Cult of Personality

7.2.1 Propaganda and the Arts

Communist Party policy in the 1920s

In the 1920s, artists, for example, Vladimir Tatlin, and writers had considerable freedom to experiment with new genres like Futurism and Modernism. Communist Party policy continued to encourage radical and progressive art and literary forms into the late 1920s, peaking in 1928–1931. The historian Martin McCauley characterises the 'glorification of the small man' in Soviet literature in the first year of the First Five Year Plan but also outlines the change in approach taken under Stalin:

Plots displayed an absence of hierarchy and experts and managers faded into the background. The machine was worshipped; indeed only a country as backward as the Soviet Union could have placed such faith in technology as the answer to man's problems. The rest of Europe had had the myth of the good machine exploded during the First World War, but for postwar Russia, noise was still a sign of progress, and the smoke belching out of factory chimneys a symbol of a brighter future.

McCauley, M. (1983) *Stalin and Stalinism*, Harlow: Longman, p. 32.

After 1931 the literary hero changes. The manager, the expert, the party official, in other words the decision-makers, take over. The writer had also to be a skilled craftsman, the "engineer of the soul", as Stalin graphically put it.

Stalinist policy: Socialist Realism

Stalin disapproved of more abstract art forms and saw art solely in propaganda terms. In 1932 Andrei Zhdanov was put in charge of the newly created Union of Soviet Writers. Zhdanov attacked 'bourgeois individualism', that is art which explored the individual's feelings and art that was not accessible to ordinary people. In the 1930s, artists had to conform to '**Socialist Realism**'; art, music, and writing were required to glorify the achievements of the Five Year Plans and Stalin's genius. Nikolai Ostrovsky's novel, *How the Steel Was Tempered*, in which the hero is a zealous member of Komsomol is typical of Socialist Realist art. Typical of the atmosphere that prevailed in the 1930s was *Pravda's* condemnation of Dimitri Shostakovitch's opera, *Lady Macbeth*, as *"muddle instead of music"*.

7.2.2 The Cult of Personality

Stalin and the other Communist Party leaders began building a cult of personality around Lenin immediately after his death, starting with the decision to embalm Lenin's body and display it in a mausoleum in Red Square in Moscow. Giant statues of Lenin were commissioned, with the first installed in Stalingrad in 1925 and in Leningrad—Petrograd was renamed Leningrad in honour of Lenin's memory—in 1926. Stalin helped promote the cult of Lenin in order to advance his own leadership claims, portraying himself as having been the Bolshevik leader closest to Lenin.

The cult of Stalin, which began with his fiftieth birthday celebrations in December 1929, when *Pravda*, the official party newspaper, devoted most of its pages to him, emphasised Stalin's indispensability to the Party and the country. From 1932, Party historians began rewriting Soviet history to discredit Stalin's rivals and enemies, such as Trotsky, as well as exaggerating Stalin's importance during the 1917 Revolution. In the film *Lenin in October* (1937), Stalin is presented as more important than Lenin in that Stalin is depicted advising Lenin on his every decision. From the 1930s onwards, pictures and statues of Stalin began to appear all over the USSR and posters of Stalin were regularly issued in runs of 150,000 or 200,000. At the May Day Parade of 1932, huge portraits of Lenin and Stalin were hung side by side in Pushkin Square in Moscow. The cult of Stalin eclipsed the cult of Lenin from the mid-1930s onwards. An excerpt from the edition of *Pravda* published in December 1939, celebrating Stalin's sixtieth birthday, conveys the extravagant terms in which the personality cult presented Stalin:

There is no similar name on the planet like the name of Stalin. It shines like a bright torch of freedom, it flies like a battle standard for millions of labourers around the world; it roars like thunder, warning the doomed classes of slave owners and exploiters…Stalin is today's Lenin! Stalin is the brain and heart of the party! Stalin is a banner of millions of people in their fight for a better life.

Key Term

Socialist Realism: from the 1930s through to the 1950s, the Party demanded that artists and writers only produce art and literature that helped promote loyalty to itself and encouraged the population to work towards creating a communist utopia.

As part of the celebrations for Stalin's sixtieth birthday, an authorised short biography of Stalin was published. In 1932–1933, 16.5 million copies of pamphlets and books written by Stalin were sold in the USSR.

The historian John Gooding has represented the cult of Stalin in the following terms:

> The cult firmed up support for the regime by presenting it in human rather than abstract ideological form; it also built up loyalty to him and put him beyond the reach of envious rivals. His image was of a stern yet just father, a man of iron will and supreme intelligence who worked ceaselessly for the general good and had unlimited concern for all who loyally served the party's aims. In his own eyes, he may well have been a successor not only to Lenin but also to Peter the Great and Ivan the Terrible, performing mighty deeds and putting enemies down with the support of an adoring multitude.

Gooding, J. (2002) *Socialism in Russia*, Basingstoke: Palgrave Macmillan.

The personality cult reached even greater heights after the Second World War, with his seventieth birthday being celebrated in 1949 with honours and titles being heaped upon him, including the title of '*Generalissimo*' and the inauguration of the Stalin Prize and Stalin Peace Prize.

7.3 The Role of Soviet Foreign Policy

7.3.1 Soviet Foreign Policy (1917–1953): An Overview

A successful foreign policy was a vital factor in both Lenin and Stalin's maintenance of power, with security a constant preoccupation for both leaders. From its inception in October 1917, through to 1941, the new Bolshevik regime in Russia found itself isolated and surrounded by hostile capitalist powers.

In Lenin's case, the Bolsheviks came to power during the First World War in which the Russians had suffered massive casualties, a large amount of Western Russia was under German military occupation and the Russian economy was in crisis. Withdrawal from the war was a priority for Lenin but Russia's former allies reacted in a hostile fashion to this decision, with several countries sending troops and supplies to Russia to aid the Whites in the Civil War.

Although foreign troops had been pulled out of Russia by the end of 1920 and the Bolsheviks won the Civil War, the new Soviet state continued to be viewed with suspicion and hostility by most European governments as well as the USA, and Japan. For Stalin, the gulf in economic development between the USSR and the hostile capitalist states of Western Europe, the USA and Japan meant that not only did he need to rapidly industrialise the USSR in order to close that gap, but he also had to conduct a foreign policy that reduced the threat of a western or Japanese attack on the USSR. In the early and mid-1930s, this resulted in Stalin trying to forge links with the western European democracies, but in 1939 Stalin abruptly abandoned this policy and signed a Non-Aggression Pact with Nazi Germany. This pact lasted until June 1941 when Hitler's invasion of the USSR saw the Soviet state face the greatest challenge in its history since 1917. The historian R.A.C. Parker evaluates the fighting on the Eastern Front between Soviet and Nazi forces in the following terms:

> This was the decisive campaign; more than anything else the survival of the Soviet Union determined the pattern of the Second World War and of the post-war world. It was the successful resistance of the Soviet Union and the victory of the Russian armies that enabled the Anglo-American coalition to join in defeating Hitler...

Parker, R. A. C. (1989) *The Second World War*, Oxford: Oxford University Press.

Stalin's diplomacy failed to prevent a Nazi invasion but the Soviet regime eventually, at the cost of a huge loss of life, was able to withstand the Nazi assault and, by 1944, liberate the country of Nazi forces. By the end of the Second World War, Stalin's own authority within the USSR was at its most secure, as Russians had rallied behind him in defence of 'Mother Russia' and Russian troops occupied large areas of Eastern Europe. Paradoxically, the Soviet authorities felt extremely vulnerable, both because of the human and economic cost of the Second World War and as a result of the economic and military might of the USA, with millions of American troops occupying large areas of Western Europe.

The opportunity provided by the Red Army's presence in Eastern Europe and the threat posed by the US military presence in Western Europe combined to lead Stalin to exert growing control over the states of Eastern Europe. This was a key cause of the onset of the Cold War. Certainly, from Stalin's perspective, the installation of Communist governments across Eastern Europe by the end of 1947 was vital to maintaining the Soviet Union's security by creating a 'buffer zone.' However, the development of the Cold War meant that Stalin continued to feel that the survival of the USSR was in the balance and led him to seek to strengthen Soviet control over Eastern Europe, extend Soviet influence across the world, maintain massive armed forces, and devote a huge proportion of expenditure to a growing nuclear arms race with the USA and its NATO allies.

7.3.2 Worldwide Revolution and Isolation (1917–1933)

Lenin and Trotsky saw revolution in international terms. When the Bolsheviks came to power in 1917, Lenin assumed that Communist revolutions would soon break out in other parts of the world. Indeed, Lenin was banking on revolutions in more advanced capitalist countries as a solution to the problem of how to create socialism in a country that was so backward in social and economic terms. Karl Marx had written that a proletarian revolution leading to the wholesale redistribution of wealth and eventually to the creation of a classless, Communist utopia, could only occur in advanced, fully industrialised societies.

In October 1917, the Bolsheviks confiscated all foreign assets in Russia. This, combined with Russia's withdrawal from the First World War following the conclusion of the Treaty of Brest-Litovsk (1918), and the apparent threat of Bolshevik ideology contaminating other countries, led to foreign intervention in the Russian Civil War on the Whites' side. As Winston Churchill put it, Britain, France, the USA, Italy, and Japan were seeking to *"strangle Bolshevism in its cradle"*. Russia's diplomatic isolation was emphasised by its absence from the Paris Peace Conference (1919) at the end of the First World War and by its initial exclusion from the League of Nations which was set up by the victor powers in 1920, chiefly France, Britain, and the USA (though the USA never joined the League). Foreign backing could not prevent the Whites' defeat in the Civil War by 1921; however, it confirmed the USSR's suspicions of the West which characterised Soviet foreign policy throughout the interwar years.

The failure of worldwide revolution and Soviet isolation

In 1919, in order to facilitate worldwide revolution and to ensure their own ascendancy over foreign Communist parties, the Bolsheviks created an international organisation of Communist parties called the Third International or Comintern (short for Communist International).

As predicted by Lenin, Communist revolutions broke out in Berlin, Bavaria, and Hungary in 1919. However, contrary to Lenin's expectations, all of these risings failed even though Bela Kun was in power in Hungary for over four months. Moreover, Lenin's assumption that Polish workers would rise up when the Red Army invaded

Poland was proved unfounded and the ensuing Russo-Polish War (1920–1921) ended in retreat and humiliation for the Bolsheviks.

'Permanent Revolution' versus 'Socialism in One Country'

With no prospect of Communist revolutions occurring elsewhere for the foreseeable future, the Soviet leadership argued furiously about the direction of its foreign policy. Trotsky was still passionately committed to organising worldwide revolution and became the main spokesman for this policy, which became known as 'Permanent Revolution'. On the other hand, Stalin promoted an alternative strategy known as 'Socialism in One Country', which argued that international revolution must be postponed and, in the meantime, the USSR had to be modernised and a socialist economy created before the USSR could seek to export socialist revolution abroad. The majority of the Party backed Stalin's policy at the Party Congress in 1925.

Trade agreements

As early as 1921, Lenin recognised the need to develop commercial links with the West in order to help rebuild Russia's shattered economy after nearly a decade of war and civil war. The search for more foreign trade was an important element in Lenin's New Economic Policy (1921). The Russian Foreign Ministry was successful in brokering trade agreements with Great Britain, Poland, Finland, Germany, and Turkey in 1921.

Isolation in the 1920s

In spite of signing trade agreements with many European countries, the USSR remained diplomatically isolated. It was not until 1924 that Great Britain officially recognised the USSR, and not until 1933 that the USA did so. The USSR did not join the League of Nations until 1934.

The two 'pariah' states come together: Russo-German relations in the 1920s

It was perhaps unsurprising that the country with which the USSR developed its closest links in the 1920s was Germany, because both countries were 'outcasts', the USSR because of its Communist ideology and its commitment to promoting worldwide revolution and Germany because of its alleged responsibility for starting the First World War. Neither was invited to join the League of Nations in 1920.

In 1922 the USSR and Germany signed the Treaty of Rapallo, which restored normal diplomatic relations and made provision for extensive commercial links between the two countries. In addition, the USSR secretly agreed that the German armed forces could train on Russian soil and that German industrialists could establish armaments factories in Russia in order to circumvent the military restrictions imposed by the Treaty of Versailles (1919). The USSR maintained close relations with Germany by signing the Treaty of Berlin in 1926, which was renewed in 1931. German engineers provided technical advice on Russian industrial projects in the 1920s.

Soviet policy towards China

Since the mid-19th century, China had been increasingly weak and vulnerable to foreign intervention and exploitation. Tsarist Russia had joined in the attempt to further its influence in China and had established a protectorate over Outer Mongolia. Russo-Japanese rivalry over Manchuria and Korea had led to the Russo-Japanese War (1904–1905). The Chinese Empire had collapsed in 1911, resulting in the country being segmented by a series of warlords. By 1921 two Chinese political parties had emerged, dedicated to reunifying China and making it a great power: The Nationalists (*Guomindang* or GMD) and the Chinese Communist Party (CCP).

The Russian leadership saw an opportunity to promote Soviet influence in China by helping one or both of these Chinese parties to overthrow the weak Beijing government which the Western governments recognised. However, there was a major dispute between Stalin and Trotsky on this issue; Trotsky favoured backing the CCP whilst Stalin believed that the CCP was too small and so argued for pressing the CCP into an alliance with the much bigger GMD.

It was Stalin's view that prevailed; Comintern provided advice, training, and money to the GMD-CCP alliance and helped broker the First United Front (1923) between them. However, Stalin's strategy proved disastrous when, in 1927, Chiang Kai-shek, the GMD leader, turned on the CCP and massacred thousands of them in the White Terror. Chiang then established himself as President of China, with the decimated remnant of the CCP licking its wounds in the remote Jiangxi province. When Mao Zedong emerged in the mid-1930s as leader of the CCP, he developed his own brand of communism and kept the CCP largely independent of Russian influence.

7.3.3 Stalin's Foreign Policy

By the early 1930s Stalin had become increasingly anxious about the possibility of facing a war on two fronts, with Germany in the West and Japan in the East.

Stalin had totally underestimated the threat of the Nazi Party in Germany until Hitler came to power in 1933. Until then, Comintern had ordered the German Communist Party (the KPD) to concentrate its attack on the Socialist Democratic Party (SPD), its main rival for working class support. This made it easier for Hitler to come to power.

Threats on Two Fronts	
The Japanese Threat	From 1931 onwards, Japan pursued an aggressive foreign policy. Having occupied Manchuria from 1931–32, Japan invaded Jehol province in China in 1933 and then launched a full-scale invasion of China in 1937. Japan signed the Anti-Comintern Pact with Nazi Germany in 1936.
	In 1939, Russian and Japanese forces fought each other at Khalkin-Gol on the Mongolian-Manchurian border, resulting in tens of thousands of casualties. This proved a decisive moment in easing Stalin's concerns about a war on two fronts, because it led to the Japanese government favouring the strategy of the South Strike Group within the Japanese armed forces who advocated an attack on the European powers' colonies in South-East Asia. The strategy of the North Strike Group, which consisted of a plan to seize Siberia from the USSR, was now dropped.
The Nazi Threat	From 1933, the USSR was confronted with the prospect of an increasingly aggressive and powerful Germany, under a regime that was extremely hostile to Communism. Hitler's ultimate goal was to achieve *"lebensraum"* (living-space) in the East at the expense of the USSR. From 1935 onwards, Hitler rapidly built up Germany's armed forces and began to undermine the restrictions placed on Germany by the Versailles Treaty. In 1938, Hitler annexed Austria and absorbed Czechoslovakia in two stages from 1938–39.

 Critical Thinking

Why did Stalin believe that the USSR was under threat in the 1930s?

 Key Term

Collective security: ensuring the security of a number of countries or of the world through international agreements obliging the signatories to act together against an aggressor state.

Stalin's search for security in the 1930s

Faced by growing threats to the USSR, at a time when it was still far behind the West in terms of industrialisation, Stalin sought to increase Soviet security by ending the USSR's diplomatic isolation. For much of the 1930s, Stalin looked to the West for '**collective security**' against the threat posed by Hitler but eventually in 1939 Stalin did a complete about-turn and signed the **Nazi-Soviet Pact.**

Underlying the twists and turns of Soviet foreign policy in the 1930s was a consistent search for security, with Stalin looking to play off the western democracies against Germany and vice-versa. Up to 1939, Maxim Litinov was the Soviet Commissar for Foreign Affairs and he favoured closer links with the West. In 1939, Stalin replaced Litinov with Vyacheslav Molotov, who preferred a deal with Nazi Germany.

 Key Term

Nazi-Soviet Pact: non-aggression pact signed by Germany and the USSR in August 1939 under which they agreed not to attack each other.

Phase one: Stalin looks to the West (1934–1939)

1934

The USSR was admitted to the League of Nations, with a permanent seat on the League's Council. The USSR signed a Non-Aggression Pact with the Baltic States.

1935

The USSR signed pacts with France and Czechoslovakia, committing itself to defend the latter against attack. However, the French government never formally ratified this agreement. At the Seventh Congress of the Communist International, Stalin's new strategy of organising an Anti-Fascist Popular Front was announced. The Popular Front involved encouraging an alliance of Communists and other left-wing parties throughout Europe to fight against Fascism. Prior to this, Comintern had worked to undermine other socialist parties, notably in Germany. In 1936–1938 a Popular Front government was in power in France, and, in 1936–1939, Spain was governed by a Popular Front coalition.

1936

Stalin sent aid to the Republicans (the government forces) in the Spanish Civil War (1936–1939). Stalin was concerned by German and Italian intervention on General Franco's side, so, from October 1936, the USSR provided the Republicans with tanks and planes and military advisers. Franco's Nationalists won in 1939.

Phase two: Stalin wavers between the Western democracies and Hitler (1938–1939)

1938

The Sudeten Crisis: in the autumn of 1938 Hitler looked poised to attack Czechoslovakia in a dispute over the German-speaking area called the Sudetenland. However, Great Britain and France were desperate to appease (conciliate) Hitler and avoid war so, at the Munich Conference in September-October 1938, they agreed to hand over the Sudetenland to Germany. The USSR was an ally of Czechoslovakia but was not invited to the Munich Conference. It is difficult to know whether Stalin would have honoured the 1935 Czech Pact if France had been willing to fight too, but what is clear is that Stalin's suspicions of Britain and France were deepened by the Sudeten Crisis. Stalin became increasingly suspicious that Britain and France were seeking to encourage Hitler to expand eastwards at Russia's expense, so that Western Europe would be left in peace.

1939

In the spring/summer of 1939, as Hitler prepared to invade Poland, Stalin considered competing diplomatic overtures from the British and French on the one hand, and the Nazis on the other. Anglo-French-Soviet talks foundered on mutual suspicions. A particular sticking-point was Stalin's insistence that the Red Army be able to send troops into Poland and Rumania in the event of a German attack. Britain and France suspected that this request was designed to bring about Soviet domination of Eastern Europe. In August 1939, Stalin decisively rejected the French-British offer of a military pact and shocked the world by getting his new Commissar for Foreign Affairs, Molotov, to conclude a Non-Aggression Pact with Nazi Germany.

---

[1] Antony Best, Jussi M Hanhimaki, Joseph A Maiolo, Kirsten E Schulze, *International History of the Twentieth Century*, London, 2004 p199

Phase three: Stalin seeks security in a pact with Hitler (1939)

1939

The Nazi-Soviet Pact (sometimes referred to as the Molotov-Ribbentrop Pact) was signed: in public it pledged both sides to friendly relations but there were secret protocols attached to it. In the secret protocols, Stalin and Hitler agreed to partition Poland. In addition, Hitler consented to Soviet expansion at the expense of Latvia, Estonia, Romania, and Finland.

Why did Stalin conclude the Nazi-Soviet Pact?

At first sight, a pact between Communist Russia and Fascist Germany appears surprising and might suggest a lack of consistency on Stalin's part. However, from Stalin's perspective this represented merely a tactical shift; his objective all along had been Soviet security, but his methods of achieving that had changed.

- The Non-Aggression Pact won the USSR a breathing-space; it bought time in which Soviet rearmament could be accelerated and the Red Army officer corps strengthened after Stalin's bloody purges of 1937–1938.
- Stalin could now look to create a **buffer zone** by expanding into the Baltic States.
- Stalin presumed that Hitler's planned invasion of Poland (September 1939) would lead to a long, drawn-out war between Germany and the western democracies, in which Germany, France, and Britain would become exhausted.

 Key Term

Buffer zone: an area keeping two hostile states apart.

Soviet Expansion (1939–1940)

Within three weeks of Hitler's invasion of Poland on 1st September 1939, Russian troops invaded Eastern Poland. Sandwiched between the *Wehrmacht* and the Red Army, Polish resistance collapsed. Germany and the USSR then divided up Poland; Western Poland, mainly inhabited by Poles, was placed under German occupation, and Eastern Poland, mainly consisting of Ukrainians, under Soviet control. In 1940 the NKVD (Soviet secret police) secretly executed about 20,000 Polish prisoners-of-war in the Katyn Forest. By late 1940, over 1 million Poles had been deported to Soviet labour camps.

In the winter of 1939–1940, Estonia, Latvia, and Lithuania were forced to sign 'mutual assistance' pacts with the USSR, resulting in their occupation by the Red Army in March 1940. Stalin also seized Bessarabia from Rumania.

The 'Winter War' (1939–1940)

Stalin sought to increase Soviet security by pushing back the Russo-Finnish border in the vicinity of Leningrad. Stalin's demand for Finnish territory was rejected and provoked a Russian invasion in November 1939. Although outnumbered by 1,000,000 to 200,000, the Finnish Army embarrassed the Red Army, which was poorly led and equipped. The Red Army's poor performance highlighted the damaging effects of the purges (1937–1938) and encouraged Hitler to think that an invasion of the USSR would be easy. Russian aggression against Finland led to the USSR's expulsion from the League of Nations.

The Russo-Japanese Non-Aggression Pact (April 1941)

Stalin's long-term nightmare of a simultaneous attack on the USSR by Germany and Japan was eased by his conclusion of a Non-Aggression Pact with Japan. The Japanese government had now abandoned the idea of expanding north at the expense of the USSR and was preparing for an offensive in South-East Asia, aimed at seizing the colonies belonging to the European colonial powers and the USA. This led to the attack on Pearl Harbor in December 1941.

Hitler's invasion of the USSR (June 1941)

Stalin became increasingly anxious about the possibility of war with Germany following Hitler's swift defeat of France, Belgium and Holland in May–June 1940 and the German invasion of Yugoslavia and Greece in the spring of 1941. However, Stalin strove desperately to postpone war with Germany, observing the terms of the Nazi-Soviet Pact by supplying Germany with oil, rubber and wheat.

In the early summer of 1941 Stalin chose to ignore warnings from both his own spies and British intelligence that Hitler was about to invade Russia; Hitler's military preparations were clear evidence of his intentions but Stalin refused to take counter-measures for fear of provoking a German attack. Consequently, when Hitler did launch a three-pronged invasion codenamed "Operation Barbarossa" in June 1941, Soviet forces were caught by surprise and Stalin was paralysed into inaction in the crucial first days of the war.

'The Great Patriotic War' (1941–1945)

Within three weeks of the invasion, over 750,000 Red Army soldiers had been captured. The poor performance of the Red Army, in spite of rearmament by Stalin which saw its size grow from 940,000 (1936) to 5 million (1941), illustrates the damage inflicted by Stalin's purge of its officer corps in 1937–1938.

The German forces were divided into three army groups: Army Group North advanced towards Leningrad, Army Group Centre advanced towards Moscow, and Army Group South's objectives were the Ukraine and Caucasus. Hitler ordered battles of encirclement to prevent Russian retreat; in July, 290,000 Russian troops were captured in the Minsk 'pocket' and 100,000 in the Smolensk 'pocket'. At first, Stalin seems to have been despondent and incapable of providing a lead but, on 3rd July, Stalin delivered a speech to the Russian people calling for a campaign of 'scorched earth' (destroying anything that could be of assistance to the Germans).

By October 1941, the *Wehrmacht* was within 100 miles of Moscow and almost half of the Soviet Union's industrial resources and arable land was under German control. By the time winter snows came in November, the Germans were in the outskirts of Leningrad and had captured the outermost tram depot in the suburbs of Moscow, but the onset of winter, for which they were unprepared, and a brilliant counter-attack in front of Moscow in December, organised by Marshal Zhukov, meant that Moscow was not captured. This was made possible by the transfer of ten Soviet divisions and 1,000 tanks from Siberia to Moscow because, by early October, Stalin was confident that there was no threat of a Japanese attack on the USSR. The Comintern agent Richard Sorge, based in Tokyo, had provided Stalin with vital intelligence about Japan's intention to attack the USA.

The Eastern Front (1942–1944)

From the beginning of 1942, the war in Russia became a war of attrition, a long slogging match. The German economy was ill-prepared for this kind of conflict. Three-quarters of Germany's casualties in the Second World War were incurred on the Eastern Front, where Russia's greater economic resources in the end told against the technologically superior Germans.

Under Stalin's Five Year Plans, many new industrial enterprises had been built in the 1930s east of the Ural Mountains and these factories and mines remained under Soviet control during the Second World War. Furthermore, between July and December 1941, over 1,500 factories and engineering plants located in Western Russia were taken apart, transported and reassembled east of the Urals.[1] An additional economic factor in the USSR's favour was that in weapons production, in contrast to Germany, the USSR focused on mass-producing a relatively small number of different models and designs, such as the excellent KV-1 and T-34 tanks which proved superior to German tanks.

In Russia, the Germans were unable to break the Red Army's defences around Moscow and Leningrad, so in 1942 they mounted an offensive southwards and eastwards towards the Transcaucasian oil fields. By August Army Group A's advance into the Caucasus was halted seventy miles short of the Caspian Sea whilst Army Group B's offensive was blocked at the Russian city of Stalingrad, which the Red Army defended with great tenacity. Hitler became obsessed with the capture of Stalingrad, partly because it was of strategic value, standing as it did on the River Volga, but undoubtedly also because it bore Stalin's name. Hitler's refusal to permit a retreat from Stalingrad was to cost the Germans over 250,000 casualties as the Russians launched a counter-offensive in November, trapping the German Sixth Army, commanded by Von Paulus, and forcing its surrender on 31st January 1943.

In January–February 1943 the Red Army resumed the offensive and pushed the Germans back to Kharkov. The Germans responded with an offensive at Kursk in July that led to the biggest tank battle in history, involving 2 million men and 6,000 tanks, and which resulted in a massive Soviet victory. The Red Army subsequently began slowly but surely to drive the Germans westwards.

1944 saw the Germans driven out of the USSR, with the siege of Leningrad lifted in January, and most of Eastern Europe was liberated as the Russians advanced towards Berlin; the Red Army advanced into Poland in March 1944 and into Romania in August 1944.

By February 1945, Russian troops were on German soil and only about 100 kilometres from Berlin, while the British and Americans had crossed the Rhine and were pushing through Western Germany. On 25th April, American and Russian soldiers met on the River Elbe.

By late April, the Red Army was laying siege to Berlin, and, on 30th April, Hitler committed suicide. On 8th May, German force surrendered.

Why did the Soviet Union defeat Nazi Germany?

- In attacking the USSR, Hitler took on an opponent which was probably unbeatable in a long conflict. Russia's vast size, the severity of the winter weather and the toughness of the Russian people defeated the Germans. The Red Army, in Churchill's phrase, *"tore the guts out of the German Army"*.

- Although the USSR suffered 3 million casualties in 1941, Stalin still had 4.2 million men in arms and more tanks and aircraft than Germany.

- After Hitler failed to defeat Russia in 1941, Germany was trapped, like in the First World War, in a war on several fronts: in North Africa, the USSR, the Balkans and, from 1943, in Italy, and from 1944, in Western Europe.

- In taking on the USSR and the USA, Hitler confronted two economic giants. In 1943, Soviet steel output was more than twice that of Germany. In 1944, the USA produced 40% of world weapon production.

- The USSR in 1928 had been behind the USA, GB, Germany and France in terms of industrial output and only just ahead of Japan; by 1940, as a result of Stalin's Five Year Plans, Soviet output was bettered only by the USA.

- The USA provided a total of between 45 and 50 billion dollars in aid (foodstuffs, industrial goods, weapons) in Lend-Lease (1941–1945) to its allies (principally Britain and the USSR).

7.3.4 Soviet insecurity at the end of the Second World War

The USSR ended the war with about 12 million troops, far more than any of the other belligerent countries, with the exception of the USA. The USSR demobilised the majority of its troops in 1945–1946, but it still retained over 4 million by 1947. The Red Army sat astride much of Central and Eastern Europe in 1945, having been drawn into the heart of Europe in liberating Nazi occupied countries and delivering the final knockout blows to Germany.

However, Stalin was acutely aware of how badly damaged the USSR had been by the war both in terms of 20-25 million Soviet deaths and the massive economic destruction; e.g. 137,000 tractors and 65,000 kilometres of railway line were destroyed, whilst 4.7 million houses were demolished. These losses explain both Stalin's determination to strip the Soviet occupation zone of Germany of its industrial plant and his desire to establish a 'buffer zone' in Eastern Europe, consisting of governments sympathetic towards the USSR.

The 'Grand Alliance' between the USSR, the USA, and Great Britain had been a 'marriage of convenience' between powers which had very different interests and ideological outlooks. Once it was clear, by 1945, that their mutual enemies, Germany and Japan, were on the point of defeat, tensions between the three powers grew rapidly. The Soviet Union came to be regarded by the USA and Great Britain as a predatory power, keen to spread communism all over Europe. On the other hand, Stalin was deeply suspicious of the USA and Britain and was anxious about the USSR's security, given how great the USSR's human and material losses had been in the Second World War.

Stalin's blockade of Berlin in 1948–1949, a breach of the **Potsdam Treaty** of 1945, which the USA, USSR and Britain signed to mark the end of the war with Germany, his retention of troops in Iran at the end of the Second World War, and his demands for territory from Turkey and for joint control of the Straits of the Dardanelles (separating the Black Sea from the Aegean Sea) all created the impression of a world-wide Communist threat. However, most historians today interpret Stalin's foreign policy in a more defensive light, motivated by insecurity and fear rather than by aggression.

At the end of the Second World War, Stalin was worried about the possibility of his former allies attacking the USSR, especially once the USA had successfully tested the A-bomb in 1945. He viewed Truman's abrupt cutting off of Lend-Lease in 1945 as evidence of US hostility. Stalin's installation of Communist governments in Eastern Europe can be seen as the consequence of such fears; he was seeking to create a defensive buffer zone against future Western attack. Furthermore, Stalin interpreted the **Marshall Plan** (1947) as an aggressive attempt by the USA to spread US influence throughout Europe—a form of 'dollar imperialism'.

Germany saw the most serious East-West confrontation; the Potsdam Treaty had divided Germany into four zones of occupation (French, British, American, and Soviet) and it soon became apparent that Stalin was totally opposed to German reunification, fearing that a united German state would ally with the West and present a huge threat to the USSR. Stalin blockaded West Berlin in 1948–1949 in an attempt to drive his former allies out of West Berlin which led the USA and Great Britain to organise a massive airlift of supplies into West Berlin. The crisis resulted in the creation of a separate (capitalist) West Germany and a separate (Communist) East Germany. During the crisis, Truman got Congress to agree to the establishment of NATO (the North Atlantic Treaty Organisation), an alliance of eleven countries (the USA, Canada, and nine European countries). This followed on from the announcement of the Truman Doctrine in 1947 in which the President pledged the USA to contain the spread of communism.

 Key Term

Potsdam Treaty: treaty signed at the end of the Potsdam Conference held in July–August 1945 to decide how the wartime allies (principally the USA, USSR, and Britain) would deal with Germany and its defeated allies at the end of the Second World War.

 Key Term

Marshall Plan: proposal put forward by George Marshall, US Secretary of State, that the USA would offer reconstruction loans to any European country requesting assistance. In 1948, sixteen western and southern European countries began to receive this aid but Stalin insisted that no eastern European country within the Soviet sphere of influence could request American aid.

The Iron Curtain

One of the key causes of the growing rift between Stalin and his former allies was the increasing Soviet control of Eastern Europe. As Stalin explained in 1945:

> This war is not as in the past. Whoever occupies a territory imposes his own social systems. Everyone imposes his own system as far as his army has the power to do so. It cannot be otherwise.

At the Yalta and Potsdam Conferences in 1945, there were heated arguments between the USSR and its American and British allies about the future government and borders of Poland and the West viewed with great suspicion Soviet intentions towards Eastern Europe as a whole. The USA was clearly worried by the emergence of the USSR as a superpower and its deployment of 11 million troops in Eastern Europe. The USA viewed the imposition of Communist governments in Eastern Europe after 1945 as evidence of Stalin's desire for unlimited expansion. This process was aided by the maintenance of Soviet troops in Eastern Europe and by the establishment of Cominform (the Communist Information Bureau) in 1947. Gradually Communist control tightened as coalition governments gave way to single party Communist regimes by 1948.

Soviet control of Eastern Europe gave rise to fears in the West that Stalin was driven by dreams of worldwide Marxist revolution and domination, that he would look to expand Soviet influence into Western Europe and other parts of the globe. Winston Churchill —out of office—made a speech in March 1946 at Fulton, Missouri in which he tried to alert the American public to the danger of the Soviet takeover in Eastern Europe. Although Churchill did concede that the USSR had the "*need to be secure on her western frontiers*", he referred to the USSR's "*expansive, proselytizing tendencies*", as an 'Iron Curtain' descended, cutting Eastern Europe off from contact with the rest of Europe.

TOPICS:
Fourth Five-Year Plan
'Hysterical isolationism'
'Zhadanovism'
The Leningrad Affair
Anti-semitism and the Doctors' Plot

All of the main features of Stalin's rule prior to the Second World War were also present in the post-war period:

- Centralised economic planning, with the introduction of the Fourth Five Year Plan, aimed at repairing the huge damage inflicted on the Soviet economy by the Second World War

- The use of terror to eliminate real and imaginary opponents and coerce the population into conformity

- Periodic purges of the Communist Party to ensure its continuing loyalty to Stalin

- The use of propaganda to take the cult of Stalin to new heights

- Continued application of the policy of Russification, including increased persecution of the Jewish population.

8.1 The Fourth Five-Year Plan (1946–1951)

Damaged factories were rapidly restored to full production capacity and railway tracks repaired or replaced. There was rapid industrial recovery, e.g. coal production in the Donets Basin by late 1947 was greater than that of 1940. Industrial recovery was helped by the seizure of industrial machinery and resources from some of the areas occupied by the Red Army at the end of the war, particularly Manchuria and the Soviet zones of Germany and Austria.

Agriculture recovered more slowly because many of the worst battles of the Second World War had taken place across the USSR's most productive land resulting in about 100,000 collective farms being destroyed and because, as in the 1930s, agriculture suffered from a lack of investment compared to industry. The 1946 grain harvest was only just half that of 1940. Just as in the 1930s, the state took very large amounts of grain in order to acquire capital to invest in industry. State procurements increased to 70% of the harvest, leading to famine in the Ukraine in 1946. In 1947 peasants were forbidden to sell their produce at market stalls. In 1948 Stalin imposed on collective and state farms a series of new agricultural techniques devised by Trofim Lysenko, including intensive planting of seed. These reforms proved disastrous.

8.2 Continuing Repression: 'Hysterical Isolationism'

The Russian historian Yuri Levada has labelled the years 1945–1953 as marked by 'hysterical isolationism'. Stalin did everything he could to prevent Soviet citizens from coming into contact with foreign influences. Russians were denied the freedom to travel abroad; very few foreigners were allowed to visit the USSR and those who did were monitored closely by the NKVD, still led by Lavrenti Beria.

Many of the Russian troops who had come into contact with the West during the Second World War were treated as possible traitors. This was particularly true of returning prisoners of war; many of them were executed or imprisoned on their return to the USSR.

The Gulag held millions of Soviet citizens during this period, including intellectuals like Alexander Solzhenitsyn who later wrote *One Day in the Life of Ivan Denisovich* about life in the Gulag.

8.3 'Zhadanovism' (1946–1948)

From 1946–1948, Andrei Zhdanov was given the task of purging artists who failed to conform to Socialist Realism. Zhadanov's approach is clearly revealed in his attack on the journals *Zvezda* and *Leningrad* published in August 1946:

> The leading workers on these journals, and primarily their editors, comrades Saianov and Likharev, have forgotten the Leninist doctrine that our journals, whether scientific or artistic, cannot be apolitical. They have forgotten that our journals are a powerful instrument of the Soviet state for educating Soviet people, the youth in particular, and must therefore be guided by that which constitutes the living foundation of the Soviet order – its politics. The Soviet order cannot tolerate its youth being educated in a spirit of indifference to Soviet politics, in a 'don't give a damn' moral vacuum.
>
> Therefore, any doctrine which is devoid of moral content and apolitical, any 'art for art's sake', is alien to Soviet literature, is damaging to the interests of the Soviet people and State, and should have no place in our journals.

The Decree of the VKP Central Committee of 14th August 1946 on the Journals *Zvezda* and *Leningrad*.

Two prominent literary targets of Zhdanov were the Leningrad poet, Anna Akhmatova, and the satirist, Mikhail Zoshchenko. Both were expelled from the Union of Soviet Writers and their works were banned. The USSR's leading composers, Shostakovich and Prokofiev, were both forced to confess to composing 'bourgeois' music and agreed to compose socialist realist music.

8.4 The Leningrad Affair (1948)

Following Zhdanov's death in 1948, there was an extensive purge of the Leningrad Communist Party, which he had been secretary of. This was expanded to a nationwide purge of thousands of party members. Historians are divided over whether this resulted from Stalin's paranoia or originated in a power struggle between a group led by Beria and Malenkov, on the one hand, and the former supporters of Zhdanov, on the other.

8.5 Anti-Semitism and the Doctors' Plot (1953)

Antisemitism increasingly became a feature of Stalin's regime after 1945. A lot of anti-semitic propaganda was produced, Jewish schools and synagogues were closed down and many Jews were arrested by the NKVD.

In January 1953, Soviet newspapers carried headlines referring to the 'Doctors' Plot'. Nine doctors (six of whom were Jews) were accused of poisoning Zhdanov and murdering other Soviet officials as part of a Western backed conspiracy. These allegations were probably intended by Stalin to serve as a pretext to increase persecution of the Jews and to initiate a fresh purge of the Party. However, this was prevented by his death in March 1953.

Under Stalin's successors in the Soviet leadership, the authoritarian system created by Lenin and maintained by Stalin, was retained, although it was done so with a much reduced degree of state violence. However, it was not until Gorbachev became Soviet leader in 1985 that the authoritarian system was fundamentally reformed. Most Western academics argue that Gorbachev's reforms in the mid to late 1980s in fact accelerated the demise of the Communist Party's monopoly of power and the collapse of the USSR in 1991.

Essay-writing Activities: The Rise and Rule of the Bolsheviks

Below, you will find two essay questions, which cover most of the issues that I have dealt with in this Revision Guide. The first answer is a model that I have created, and the second is a very good answer by a student that I have suggested could be improved in certain ways. By examining these questions, you will be able to test your understanding and recall of Soviet history, and gain insights into how to construct responses to IB essay questions.

For the first example, I have given you some ideas about how the question could be tackled and then provided you with space to add examples and further points.

1. **"Authoritarian states achieve power as the result of a revolutionary process against tradition." Does this adequately explain the acquisition and consolidation of power by one authoritarian state that you have studied?**

In answering this question, using the Bolsheviks' establishment of an authoritarian state in Russia, do not be put off by its wording, in particular the phrase 'revolutionary process against tradition'. Firstly, point out that the Bolsheviks were Marxists and, as such, they sought to overthrow the traditional ruling classes and social system in Russia. This they achieved in the period 1917–1921 by means of the October Revolution and the Civil War. However, it is necessary also to examine the February Revolution, which overthrew the traditional system of government in Russia and which involved a popular revolutionary movement. Arguably the Bolsheviks hijacked this popular revolutionary process for their own ends. Finally, think about the key word 'adequate'. Clearly, the events of 1917–1921 can be viewed to a considerable extent as 'a revolutionary process against tradition' but there were also other factors, which enabled the Bolsheviks to seize power and consolidate it up to 1921.

I have divided my answer in two parts. In the first I have outlined the ways in which the Bolshevik acquisition of power can be explained by reference to a 'revolutionary process against tradition'. In the second, I have considered the ways in which that does not provide an 'adequate' explanation. I have left space for you to provide your own points and examples/evidence.

> **To some extent, "yes".**
> - Marxism aims at the overthrow of social hierarchy; in Russia, this meant the Tsar, noble landowners, and industrialists. In *What Is To Be Done?* (1902), Lenin argued that the Bolsheviks must act as a vanguard party to lead a proletarian revolution.
> - The fall of The Monarchy in the February Revolution of 1917 can be seen as a revolt against tradition. The traditional form of government (Tsarism) had been discredited by its military, political and economic shortcomings in the First World War. However, the February Revolution was not brought about by the Bolsheviks but by the workers of Petrograd, joined by soldiers of the Petrograd garrison; the Duma felt obliged to acknowledge the Petrograd Soviet and accept the fall of The Monarchy (the Duma members would have preferred to have exchanged Nicholas II for an alternative Tsar).
>
> *(continued)*

To some extent, "yes". *(continued)*

- Lenin's *April Theses* constituted a manifesto for revolutionary change. Lenin controversially argued for a second revolution. He rejected the notion of bourgeois parliamentary government as insufficiently revolutionary. Government by the traditional ruling classes had to be replaced by a soviet/workers' government; Russia should be immediately withdrawn from the First World War as it was an imperialist war.

- One of the key reasons for the Bolsheviks' growing support in 1917 was that Lenin rejected any idea of compromise with the propertied classes, whereas the other socialist parties, the Mensheviks and Social Revolutionaries, continued to support the Provisional Government.

- Even before October 1917, a popular revolution was underway, characterised by the establishment of Soviets, workers' seizure of factorys and peasant seizure of land from the nobles. In the view of historians like Orlando Figes, the Bolsheviks hijacked this popular revolution and distorted it for their own ends. This is how the Kronstadt rebels who rose against the Bolsheviks saw it in 1921.

- The October Revolution, to some extent, depended on the Bolsheviks' harnessing the revolutionary mood of the workers and garrison soldiers. The Petrograd Soviet and Red Guards supported the overthrow of the Provisional Government because they felt it did not represent their interests whereas the Bolsheviks promised the overthrow of the traditional order. Lenin created a new type of government, Sovnarkom, a socialist coalition (the Bolsheviks and Left SRs), to replace the Duma-based government that the Provisional Government essentially had been.

- Sovnarkom's first measures, to an extent, represented a revolution against tradition: it issued decrees allowing peasants to take land from the nobles, church and Tsar; it empowered workers to set up factory committees to take control of factories.

- During the Civil War, the Bolsheviks implemented policies which undermined the traditional order and these, to an extent, contributed to their consolidation of power. War Communism (1918–1921) involved nationalisation of all factories. The Bolsheviks murdered the royal family in 1918 in order to prevent the Whites ('traditional' forces) from using them as a rallying point. Lenin set up Comintern (1919) to promote worldwide revolution and the overthrow of 'tradition' internationally. The Bolsheviks attacked 'traditional' beliefs in the shape of the Orthodox Church and fought the Whites who represented the landowners and Tsarist officers – i.e. the old order.

Your points FOR the statement:

_____

_____

_____

_____

_____

_____

BUT not an 'adequate' explanation because:

- The February Revolution (which made the October Revolution possible) was a limited revolution against tradition—it saw the transfer of political power to the educated classes (Duma) and it was made to a considerable extent by the elites (generals, Duma) deserting the Tsar.

- Some of the Bolsheviks' early measures were not that 'revolutionary', e.g. the Decree on Land (October 1917) was not Marxist because it allowed peasants to enlarge their private holdings of land.

- During the Civil War, the Bolsheviks could be very pragmatic; Trotsky and Lenin used the forces of tradition in their war against the Whites, e.g. the Bolsheviks employed 50,000 ex-Tsarist officers and brought back many former managers to run factories. Lenin and Trotsky rejected 'revolutionary warfare' and instead raised a conscript army (5 million).

Other factors contributed to the Bolsheviks' acquisition and consolidation of power:

- Both the February and October Revolutions were the product of intense crises brought about by Russia's inability to fight successfully against a more modernised Germany in the First World War.

- The workers of Petrograd were primarily protesting about food shortages and inflation, not 'tradition' (though they held Nicholas II's government responsible).

- The October Revolution was the **product of other factors** too; e.g. Lenin's flexibility in revising Marx's ideas and persuading the Bolsheviks that a proletarian revolution was possible in a relatively backwards Russia. The Kornilov Affair undermined the Provisional Government, as did its inability to manage the war and the economy.

- The Bolsheviks' victory in the Civil War was also **due to other factors**: e.g. the divisions among the Whites, the geopolitical advantages of the Reds (control of the heart of the railway network, more cohesive territory).

- Even after the Civil War, the Bolsheviks realised that in order to stay in power they could not reject 'tradition' entirely, or, at least, not yet. Lenin introduced the New Economic Policy, which represented a retreat from socialism; private profit was permitted in the countryside and small industries could be privately owned.

- The Bolsheviks did not feel strong enough to take on 'tradition' in the countryside in the form of peasant ownership of farmland until 1929 when the 'real' revolution occurred with the 'revolution from above', in the form of collectivisation. Equally, only in 1928 did the Bolsheviks completely end 'traditional' patterns of private ownership of industry when the First Five Year Plan was launched.

Your points AGAINST the statement:

_____

_____

_____

_____

_____

_____

Conclusion

Yes, the Bolshevik acquisition of power is adequately explained by reference to a revolutionary process against tradition because the Bolsheviks were consciously seeking to overthrow the traditional order in Russia. In 1917, under Lenin's leadership, the Bolsheviks aimed at wholesale change that would destroy the power and wealth of Russia's propertied classes. To a considerable extent, the Bolsheviks capitalised on a growing popular movement, particularly in the shape of the Soviets, to seize power and retain it. The Bolsheviks then distorted the revolutionary process in Russia by creating a ruthless single party dictatorship, instead of allowing the people to take power themselves. Although an adequate explanation, the statement does not provide a full explanation of why the Bolsheviks achieved power. For that, it is necessary to consider the crisis facing Russia by 1917 and other factors such as the leadership of Lenin and Trotsky and the weaknesses of the Provisional Government and of the Whites.

1. **Examine the methods used by which one 20th century leader of an authoritarian state maintained his power.**

A student's answer:

After Stalin had achieved control of the Soviet Communist Party by 1928, he was faced with the task of maintaining his power both inside and outside the Party. Stalin's ability to judge the mood of the Party, as shown by his abandonment of NEP and adoption of the Five Year Plans and collectivisation, was a key factor in his retention of his authority over the party. Furthermore, the imposition of this 'revolution from above' gave the Communist Party unprecedented control over both the rural and urban population. Arguably, without rapid industrialisation, the USSR would not have been able to withstand Hitler's invasion in 1941, and therefore the Communist Party's power would not have survived. Stalin's use of propaganda and his encouragement of a personality cult were also vital in generating positive support. However, the most important method used by Stalin was his use of terror; the purges ensured the co-operation and loyalty of the Soviet public and the Party, the latter essentially being totally remodelled in the process.

Stalin's implementation of collectivisation played an important role in generating Party support as well as helping Stalin gain greater control over the peasantry. 'Dekulakisation' in 1929–1930 involved attacking the '*kulaks*' who were seen by many in the Party as 'petty bourgeoisie'; therefore, Party members saw collectivisation as a step away from the compromise with capitalism that NEP represented and towards the creation of a classless society and so encouraged many to see Stalin as committed to communist values and increased their support for him. The peasants, however, were meant to see 'dekulakisation' as a warning of the consequences of not co-operating with the Party. This was partly unsuccessful with regards to the suppression of the peasantry as in 1929–1930 peasants slaughtered their livestock. That said, Stalin did achieve greater control over the grain supply with procurements rising from 15% in 1928 to a peak of 40% in 1933, which helped cement his popularity within the Party. However, there were still food shortages and bread rationing in the cities until the mid-1930s and the disruption caused by the brutal liquidation of the *kulaks* seems to have led some leading figures in the Party, such as Riutin, to question Stalin's leadership, to the point of considering replacing him, possibly with Kirov. The establishment of collective farms also strengthened the Party's control over much of the Soviet population because each collective farm had a Party official as its chairman and NKVD units were stationed at Motor Tractor Stations. Previously the peasantry had been dispersed in 24 million individual farms and hardly any had belonged to the Communist Party—fewer than 0.01% of peasant families had a single Party member in 1928.

Many historians have argued that Stalin's rapid industrialisation programme was essential to the survival of the communist regime. Certainly, fear about the USSR's vulnerability to foreign invasion motivated Stalin's introduction of the Five Year Plans, as shown by his claim in 1931 that the USSR had ten years to close the gap with the more advanced capitalist countries or face destruction. Estimates of Soviet industrial growth vary and official Soviet figures were grossly inflated but Western historians believe that Soviet industry grew at somewhere between 7% and 14% per year during 1928–1940. The USSR in 1928 had been behind the USA, Britain, Germany and France in terms of industrial output and only just ahead of Japan; by 1940 Soviet output was bettered only by the USA. Arguably without this expansion the USSR's victory over Nazi Germany in 1941–1945 would not have been possible. Moreover, the Five Year Plans did inspire many Russians, particularly within Komsomol, to help on building projects, most famously the construction of Magnitogorsk, which demonstrated the belief in Stalin that many young Russians had. However, his policy of 'iron discipline', whilst demoralising many, had the effect of scaring the Russian population in to submission. Furthermore, the reintroduction of internal passports—abolished in 1917—gave the Party much tighter control over the movement of the urban population.

> **Such as?**

The use of propaganda and the creation of a cult of Stalin's personality helped maintain his dominance over the Party and his authority over the Soviet population. The cult of the leader, which began in 1929, emphasised Stalin's indispensability to the Party and the country. From 1932, Party historians began rewriting Soviet history to discredit Stalin's rivals and enemies, such as Trotsky, as well as exaggerating Stalin's importance during the 1917 Revolution. Stalin also imposed much greater restrictions on artists and writers, insisting that all art conformed to 'Socialist Realism' which would glorify the Five Year Plans, 'heroes of socialist labour' such as Stakhanov and, above all, Stalin's 'genius'. This contrasted with Lenin's tolerance of more experimental art in the early 1920s. **In line with this more repressive attitude, Stalin intensified persecution of both the Orthodox Church and Muslim communities, closing down 95% of mosques.**

> **This sentence has not been linked to the question.**

Stalin's Great Terror of 1936–1938, as with Lenin's earlier purges, was designed to keep the Party disciplined and committed. **However, Stalin's purges were far more savage and seemed to be motivated by Stalin's paranoia and desire to maintain his own personal authority.** In 1934 Sergei Kirov received more votes in the Central Committee elections than Stalin, shortly afterwards he was assassinated and Stalin used his murder to justify the purges. Stalin used the purges to maintain power by permanently removing his enemies and rivals within the Party, for example, eliminating Zinoviev and Kamenev in 1936 and the 'Trotskyite-Rightists' in 1938. Furthermore, over the course of the Great Terror approximately

> **Given that this factor is being put forward as the most important in maintaining Stalin's power, it could have been developed more fully.**

600,000 Party members were executed and 1 million purged; in effect, Stalin created a new party, instilled with loyalty to him personally. Outside of the Party, over half of the senior army officers were executed and millions of ordinary Soviet citizens imprisoned within the *Gulag* system. This created a powerful climate of fear which terrorised the population in to submission. However, Revisionist historians such as Arch Getty have questioned the extent to which Stalin really did control the Soviet population, suggesting that the purges, once initiated by Stalin, got out of control and gained a momentum of their own, driven from below.

In conclusion, it was Stalin's use of terror that above all helped him maintain his power. Other factors did play a role, such as his 'Revolution from above' in the 1930s, transforming the USSR in to a far more industrialised country, creating the economic basis for Soviet victory in the Second World War. Propaganda and the cult of personality contributed to both boosting Stalin's popularity and creating an illusion of popularity. Nonetheless, it seems that, for Stalin, terror acted as the most effective method of maintaining power, strengthening his hold over the Communist Party and intimidating the population into submitting to its authority.

> **Differing historical perspectives: the answer above makes brief reference to differing historical interpretations but this could have been usefully expanded.**

Image Credits

Figure 4.1   *Trotsky.*
Source: The Russian Bolshevik Revolution (Century Co, New York: 1921), via Wikimedia Commons [public domain] (File uploaded by user: INeverCry)

Figure 4.2   *Stalin.*
Source: State museum of political history of Russia [CC BY-SA 3.0], via Wikimedia Commons (File uploaded by user: Soerfm)

IBDP REVISION COURSES

Summary

Who are they for?
Students about to take their final IBDP exams (May or November)

Locations include:
Oxford, UK
Rome, Italy
Brussels, Belgium
Dubai, UAE
Adelaide, Sydney & Melbourne, AUS
Munich, Germany

Duration
2.5 days per subject
Students can take multiple subjects

The most successful IB revision courses worldwide

Highly-experienced IB teachers and examiners

Every class is tailored to the needs of that particular group of students

Features

- Classes grouped by grade (UK)
- Exam skills and techniques – typical traps identified
- Exam practice
- Pre-course online questionnaire to identify problem areas
- Small groups of 8–10 students
- 24-hour pastoral care.

Revising for the final IB exams without expert guidance is tough. Students attending OSC Revision Courses get more work done in a shorter time than they could possibly have imagined.

With a different teacher, who is confident in their subject and uses their experience and expertise to explain new approaches and exam techniques, students rapidly improve their understanding. OSC's teaching team consists of examiners and teachers with years of experience – they have the knowledge and skills students need to get top grades.

The size of our Oxford course gives some particular advantages to students. With over 1,000 students and 300 classes, we can group students by grade – enabling them to go at a pace that suits them.

Students work hard, make friends and leave OSC feeling invigorated and confident about their final exams.

We understand the needs of IBDP students – our decades of experience, hand-picked teachers and intense atmosphere can improve your grades.

"I got 40 points overall, two points up from my prediction of 38, and up 7 points from what I had been scoring in my mocks over the years, before coming to OSC. Thank you so much for all your help!"

OSC Student

Please note that locations and course features are subject to change - please check our website for up-to-date details.

Find out more: 🏠 osc-ib.com/revision 📱 +44 (0)1865 512802

MID IBDP SUMMER PROGRAMMES

Summary

Who is it for?
For students entering their final year
of the IB Diploma Programme

Locations include:
Harvard and MIT, USA
Cambridge, UK

Duration
Min. 1 week, max. 6 weeks
1 or 2 IB subjects per week

Improve confidence and
grades

Highly-experienced IB
teachers and examiners

Tailored classes to meet
students' needs

Wide range of available
subjects

Safe accommodation and
24-hour pastoral care

Features

- Morning teaching in chosen IB subject
- 2nd IB subject afternoon classes
- IB Skills afternoon classes
- One-to-one Extended Essay Advice,
  Private Tuition and University Guidance
  options
- Small classes
- Daily homework
- Unique IB university fair
- Class reports for parents
- Full social programme.

By the end of their first year, students understand the stimulating and challenging nature of the IB Diploma.

They also know that the second year is crucial in securing the required grades to get into their dream college or university.

This course helps students to avoid a 'summer dip' by using their time effectively. With highly-experienced IB teachers, we consolidate a student's year one

learning, close knowledge gaps, and introduce some year two material.

In a relaxed environment, students develop academically through practice revision and review. They are taught new skills, techniques, and perspectives – giving a real boost to their grades. This gives students an enormous amount of confidence and drive for their second year.

"The whole experience was incredible. The university setting was inspiring, the friends I made, and the teaching was first-class. I feel so much more confident in myself and in my subject.

OSC Student

Please note that locations and course features are subject to change - please check our website for up-to-date details.

Find out more: osc-ib.com/mid +44 (0)1865 512802